GENEALOGICAL ABSTRACTS
FROM THE
South Carolina Gazette

1732–1735

COMPILED BY *Alton T. Moran*

HERITAGE BOOKS
2014

I0100049

HERITAGE BOOKS
AN IMPRINT OF HERITAGE BOOKS, INC.

Books, CDs, and more—Worldwide

For our listing of thousands of titles see our website
at
www.HeritageBooks.com

Published 2014 by
HERITAGE BOOKS, INC.
Publishing Division
5810 Ruatan Street
Berwyn Heights, Md. 20740

International Standard Book Numbers
Paperbound: 978-1-55613-070-0
Clothbound: 978-0-7884-6033-3

FOREWORD

Although my review of the Gazette was undertaken for purely genealogical and historical research purposes. I could not help but be fascinated with the surprisingly rich social and cultural life of the people in this area of our country in these early pre-revolutionary War times. I know of no other source that provides such an incisive look into their lives as this newspaper.

The Gazette was founded in 1732 and our compilation begins with the initial issue. According to a contemporary issue of *Gentleman's Magazine*, Charleston at this time consisted of "between 500 and 600 Houses . . . the most of which are very costly, besides 5 handsome churches," and "it was a place where the people except those who give themselves up to debauchery, are all rich, either in slaves, furniture, cloathes, plate, jewels, or other merchandise . . . ."

A reader of this compilation will learn the inhabitants of many of these 500-600 houses, he will see that there was richness (by 18th Century standards) and that there was also some debauchery. In preparing this compilation, I have attempted to record all excerpts from the Gazette containing a name of an inhabitant of the region, if the excerpt appeared more than once I have recorded only the first entry. Although all names have been recorded, some of the excerpts have been condensed. I have also offered substitutes for some of the more archaic words, but only when absolutely necessary. The reader will also notice that the spelling of some words, especially proper names, is often inconsistent. In these instances I have not substituted my own judgment, but have remained truthful to the original spellings as they appear in the *Gazette*.

In 1731 the South Carolina General Assembly offered a bounty of Ł1000 to obtain a printer for the colony. At this time seven colonial communities already had presses and four had newspapers, i.e., Boston, Philadelphia, New York and Annapolis. Three men, George Webb, Eleazer Phillips and Thomas Whitmarsh proceeded to Charleston to compete for the bounty. George Webb, perhaps the first South Carolina printer died not long after arriving in Charleston. The other two issued South Carolina's first newspapers, Whitmarsh with the *Gazette* which appeared on January 8, 1732 and Phillips with the *South Carolina Weekly* which began at about the same time. As no issues remain, its time of existence is based on only two advertisements which appeared in the *Gazette* on January 13, 1733 and March 22, 1735.

Thomas Whitmarsh was an English printer who met Benjamin Franklin in London and came to Philadelphia between 1726 and 1729 to work with him. Whitmarsh worked for Franklin until the summer of 1731 when he left for Charleston. Beside printing the Gazette, Whitmarsh printed pamphlets, broadsides and a variety of legal forms. He also sold office supplies, and books. Whitmarsh continued his business relationship with Franklin until his death on September 20 or 21 in 1733.

The *Gazette* was discontinued until February 2, 1734 when another associate of Franklin's, Lewis Timothee' (later Timothy) became its editor. Timothee' was the son of a French protestant refugee, who had left France and moved to Holland. By 1731, Timothee' with his wife Elizabeth (who was born and lived in Holland) and four children, Peter, Louis, Charles, and Mary (all under six years of age) were residing in Philadelphia. The family resided in Front Street, next door to Dr. Kearsley. Timothee' first worked for Franklin as editor of the *Philadelphische Zeitung* which was intended for Philadelphia's German population. When this publication ceased Timothee', with Franklin's assistance, became librarian of the Philadelphia Library Company on November 14, 1732. On November 28, 1733 Timothee' and Franklin entered into an agreement by which Timothee' was put into the printing business in Charleston with Franklin receiving one-third of the profits of the business. Timothee' wasted no time resuming the printing business in Charleston, publishing the Gazette on February 2, 1734. He continued as editor until his death in December 1738.[1]

1. *The South Carolina Gazette* by Henning Cohen, University of South Carolina Press, 1953.

NEWSPAPER ABSTRACTS - 1732

8 January 1732

South Carolina *Gazette* printed by **Thomas Whitemarsh** at house of **Mr. Hugh Evans**, Tailor in Church Street.

W. Saxby advertises for two stray horses which he describes.

15 January 1732

A fire broke out in **Mr. Van Velsen's** back shop.

22 January 1732

Died - **George Keith** on Sunday last at 2:00 in prison believed to have been murdered. However an inquest determined that he died of natural causes. Two surgeons stated his death was caused by his intemperate way of living.

Married - **Christiana Broughton**, daughter of the **Honorable Colonel Broughton**, President of His Majesty's Council of this Province was married to the **Rev. Mr. Dwight**.

Hugh Evans advertises for dog lost on the 12th.

29 January 1732

John Herbert - Commissioner for Indian Affairs introduces Cherokee Indians to His Excellency.

Charles James pursued a runaway Negro, who had robbed him, fought him, and struck his musket against his skull, killing him. He told a Justice what he had done. The Justice ordered the Negro's head cut off and fixed to a pole and put up near Ashley Ferry.

Stephen Proctor has a store on Mr. Wragg's Bridge where can be purchased salt made by **Mr. Millichamp**.

5 February 1732

Mishap occurred to Sloop *Dolphin* during her voyage from North Carolina for the Island of Mountiferat. **Thomas Pilson**, Master and Owner, **Tho. Etheritlge**, Mate, **Rich Banks**, **Wedington R. Rance**, **Mich. Jones**, **S. Brandin** and a Negro named **R y a n**, Sailors. At Lat. of 25, 30 N. Lat. and 63, 39 W. Long. ship wrecked. **Rance** drowned, the rest got on side of the wreck. They were rescued over 21 days later. [Article describes their ordeal.] Surgery on **Rich Evans** was performed by **Mr. George Valentine**, Surgeon on H.M.S. *Fox*.

Ball of fire seen about 4 miles from the town.

Raffle to be held at house of **Mrs. Surrow**.

Tho. Philips runs ad for return of stolen clothes and goods taken from off his horse between Charlestown and the Quarter House.

Thomas Bartram advertises for sale of his billiard table at his house on Charlestown Green.

Thomas Binford intends to depart this province and wants to settle accounts.

To Be Sold the personal estate of **M r . J o h n G o d f r e y**, deceased. Includes 42 Negroes (some of them Tradesmen) horses, cattle, etc. Sale to be made at his plantation lying near Wappoo Bridge between Stono and Ashley Rivers. Ad run by **Benjamin Whitaker**.

12 February 1732

To Be Sold a house and plantation, about six miles from Charles Town, commonly called the Quarter-House. Contact **John Laurens**, Saddler.

19 February 1732

Mr. Gough was killed this week by a gentleman who has the misfortune to be out of his senses.

Issac Mazyck, Jr., advertises plantation for sale on the south side of the Santee River.

All persons indebted to **Mr. Tho. Monck**, merchant are desired to pay the same to **Mr. George Austin**, Merchant.

Estate of the late **Rev. Mr. Ludlam**, advertised for sale by **William Dry**, administrator.

Edmond Atkin intends to depart Charlestown and wants to settle accounts.

Runaway from his Master, **John Fisher** at Will Town, a white servant named **Calet Lowle**, aged about 18, by trade a Taylor having on a red Whitney coat. He is a slim lad with a round pale face.

Runaway: a Pauper Negro woman, formerly of the Estate of **Mr. Giles Cooke**, deceased. Contact **John Mortimer** in Christ-Church Parish.

26 February 1732

Reward offered by **William Linthwaite** for return of large packet of letters taken from the shop of **Mr. Clifford**, including paper directed to **John Colleton**, Esq. of Farlawns.

All persons indebted to **Samuel Martyn**, peruke maker, are directed to pay same to **Mr. Stephen Proctor** as **Mr. Martyn** is leaving for Great Britain.

The Commissioners appointed to issue out public orders for discharging the debts of the province meet every Wednesday in the house of **Col. Miles Brewton**.

J. Townsend advertises that any who are indebted to him should pay him directly and not his Negroes or any other person.

Mary Wood, wife of **John Wood**, of St. Andrew's Parish has left her husband.

All persons indebted to the estate of **William Cheatham**, deceased, are desired to pay their debts to **Mr. John Champney**. Ad run by **Benjamin Whitaker**.

To be sold, the personal estate of **Mr. Hill Cross**, deceased, at his dwelling house, commonly called the Quarter House. Executors **Ed Cross** and **Charles Pinckney**.

Charles Hargrave - Master of the Ship *Dragon*.

4 March 1732

Runaway: Negro boy named **London**. Reward offered by his master **James Granes**.

All persons who have demands on the Estate of **Maj. David Durham** are desired to contact **James Crokatt** of Charlestown of **Issac Child**, of Strawberry.

Hugh Swinton has for sale nice land in Childsberry Town.

Gilison Clapp offers to lease or sell a brick house 40 X 30 fronting the river at Dorchester.

Benjamin Whitaker offers for sale property lying next to plantations of **Charles Hill** and **Benjamin Godfrey**.

All persons indebted to the estate of **John Wright**, deceased are desired to pay **Mr. Ribton Hutchinson** or **Richard Woodward** of Charlestown. Ad run by **Andrew Rutledge**.

Mr. Gouiran offers reward for return of his lost dog, Cupid.

William Webb of James Island advertises for return of lost canoe.

11 March 1732

Charles Burnham, executor of estate of **Charles Burnham**, deceased, as well as guardian to his children.

Reward offered for return of Negro named **B e t t y** belonging to **Mrs. Catherine Cattell** on Ashley River. Contact **William Cattell, Jr.** or **John Champly** in Charlestown.

To Be Sold – plantation lying at Wampera in St. John's Parish, where **Mr. William Bertson**, deceased, formerly lived.

To Be Let or Sold – a plantation on James Island lying on Newtown Creek, joining on the **Widow Stow**, **Mr. James Taylor** and **Capt. Laurence Dennis**. Apply to **Col. Arthur Hall**, **Capt. Tho. Howard**, or **Mr. Will Chapman** on James Island. If not sold before the 6th of April, it will be sold that day, by public vendue at house of **Mr. Samuel Drake** on the same island.

18 March 1732

William Cattell and **Tobias Fitch**, administrators of estate of **William Cantey**, deceased.

Sale of slaves at the late plantation of **Mr. William Donning** near Dorchester.

All persons who have demands on the estate of **Mr. John Williams** of James Island, deceased, are desired to bring their accounts to **Paul Hamilton**, **Joseph Stanyarn**, **William Wilkins, Jr.**, and ---- **Wilkins**, Relict and Executrix.

James De'Veaux, Cutter, two doors below **Col. Prioleau** in Church Street makes razors, knives, swords, etc.

25 March 1732

Trial of **Joseph Summers**, indicted as accessory to burglary and robbery committed by **Peter French**. Found Guilty and order given to construct a gallows, **Robert Wright**, Chief Justice of the Province, **Eleazar Allen**, Cooper, and **Tweedie Somerville**, Assistant Judges.

Haynes, who was sent to the parsonage on account of smallpox is doing well. No other cases in or near this town.

Nicholas Haynes offers reward for return of strayed horse.

Dwelling house of **Richard Eagle** of Charlestown was burglarized and much stolen.

Blacksmith tools for sale by **Thomas Lovelace**.

All persons indebted to Estate of **Robert Buchanan**, Shipkeeper, deceased are desired to discharge these debts. **Charles Pinckney**.

1 April 1732

Between the hours of 11 and 12 on Thursday last, **Joseph Somers** was executed. His wife and child went with him to the Gallows where he took his last farewell of them. He denied, to the last, that he was Guilty of the crime for which he was charged, but acknowledged that he had often committed other crimes for which he deserved death and that Lying, Swearing, Theft, Whoring, and general neglect of divine ordinances were his vices. His parents died when he was not yet a year old, he was left in the Parish where he was born near Sherborne in Dorsetshire, and in 1699 put out to a shoemaker. At age 14 he left his Master and went to sea in the King's and the Merchant Service until he came to this colony. Maintains he was not guilty of the charges alleged, namely blowing up Magazine or the Death of **George Keith**.

A violent storm leveled many trees on plantation of **Mr. Moses Bennet**.

Joseph Haynes dies of smallpox on Tuesday last, the 17th day after being taken ill.

Thomas Cole, died of a flu at home of **Stephen Beaton. Mr. Cole** came to this town six months ago for his health. He left a will leaving most of his possessions to a brother in England. Possessions included 727 ounces of silver, plus gold and other items.

Quit-rents due to his Majesty shall be paid to me **A. Skene**, or **Alexander Stewart**, my Deputy, at my Office in Charlestown and persons holding lands in Craven or Granville Counties are to pay **William Swinton** at Winyaw or **Thomas Wigg** at Port Royal.

Sale of land on the Bay - **Eleazar Allen**.

Strayed or took from under **Mr. Thomas Elliot's** Bridge, a long boat. Reward offered by **Adam Beauchamp**.

Two plantations to be sold, one containing 355 acres on Wando Neck, 12 miles from Charlestown. The other containing 700 acres, on Santee River called the Peach Tree. Both by **Eliz. Boon** living at **Mr. Hixts** on Wando Neck. Contact **Mrs. Elizabeth Croxson** in Charlestown.

Eloped from her husband, **Philip Lovett**, on the 22nd of March last, **Mary Lovett**, her maiden name **Carpenter** and took goods with her.

Sophia Lienbrey no longer lives with her husband, **Peter Lienbrey**.

Runaway - a Negro man named **Owen** belonging to **Mr. Abraham Muffins**. He had been sold by estate of late **Mr. John Godfrey**. Reward offered for return to his Master living in Goose Creek near **Mr. Lamedan Smith**.

6

Stolen or strayed from Charlestown, a dark bay mare and the sign of the Green Ball, supposed to be blown down by the wind. Reward offered by **Anne Morgan** in Charlestown.

To be sold: a plantation near the mouth of Goose Creek adjoining to **Mr. Vander Dussen's** Plantation. Inquire of **Mr. Job Howes** or **Mr. J. Clifford.**

Seventy acres for sale, most of oak and hickory, joining on **Mr. Codnor** and **Mr. John Daniel.** Contact **Mr. Charles King** at Cainhoy or **Mr. Robert Austin** in Charlestown.

8 April 1732

To be sold: a handsome coach and harness - Inquire of **Robert Johnston** in Charlestown. Also 22 acres in St. Thomas Parish near the Church, 18 miles from Charlestown.

Pine lumber to be sold by **Mr. Will.** Dry from his plantation by the Quarter House.

On Monday last, after a very long disorder, died **M r s .** Mazyck, wife of **Mr. Issac Mazyck, Sr.,** merchant of this town, in an advanced age. She was interred in the Churchyard of this place.

Ships who sailed: *The Solebay*; **C a p t . P e t e r W a r r e n ,** Commander; *The Embleton*, **John Payne**, Master.

Whereas the dwelling house of **Mr. Richard Eagle** of Charlestown has been lately broken open. Offers a reward for information on robbers.

15 April 1732

Runaway from **Tho. Heyward** on James Island, a Negro woman named **Betsy**, aged 19, a lusty wench and speaks good English, being born in the province. Reward offered. Return to **Mr. Ellis**, Constable of Charlestown.

Peter Verges, Confectioner, at the house of **Mrs. Valette** on the Bay sells all sorts of confectionaires, both dry and moist.

Edward Wigg sells books in Charlestown (contains long list).

Robert Austin and **William Mackenzie** chosen church wardens.

7

A Negro child belonging to **Mr. Bampfield**, the Provost Martial was taken ill with the smallpox and removed to the Parsonage.

Mr. Osmond, Merchant of this town was married to Miss **Mary Hall**, daughter of Col. **Arthur Hall** of this province. A young lady of great wealth and fortune.

A cypress canoe called the *Old Dolphin* taken from C o l. **Brewton's** bridge. Canoe formerly belonged to **Mr. Quelch** of Hobkoy. Reward offered by **Edw. Scrull** of Charlestown.

23 April 1732

All persons indebted to the estate of **James McNabney**, deceased, are desired to pay the same to **Mesrs. Andrew Allen, John Frazier** and **George Ducat. By Richard Allen**

Strayed from the plantation of **Arthur Middleton** at Crofield, a bright bay horse. Whoever brings the horse to **Mr. Brandt's** in Charlestown will receive a pound reward.

Eight men are wanted for the Scout Boat under the command of Capt. **William Furguson** by **Alexander Parris**, Commissary.

To be sold: by **William Osborne** and **Helena**, his wife, two islands, within twelve miles of Port Royal. One containing 2000 acres of good land to raise stock on and commonly known as Mackeys Island. The smaller island contains 450 acres and lies contiguous to the other.

A tract of land containing 500 acres at Winyaw joining upon Waccremaw River. Contact **Peter Girardeau** at Ashley River.

Festival of St. George's Day deferred to the day following when the company of Fort Jolly volunteers, consisting of 25 able men, met at the house of **Trooper Pointsett**, their usual house of rendezvous, and were delayed by difficulties after embarking for here. No men were killed though one was wounded.

30 April 1732

Strayed out of **Mr. Brandt's** pasture, about nine months ago, a bay horse. Contact **Issac Lewis** of Charlestown or **John Ouldfield** in Goose Creek.

On Monday morning last died **Mr. William Hammerton,** Naval Officer for this Port arrived here from England, his brother, in order to enter upon the Post of Secretary of this Province.

On Thursday last, about eight in the evening, **Doctor William Clelland** was married to **Mrs. McNabney,** a Widow lady of good fortune at her house in the town.

A muster of two foot companies of the Militia was held. One commanded by **Capt. Robert Brewton** and the other by **Capt. Adam Beauchamp.**

John Hammerton took oath as Secretary of this Province.

Nathanial Braughton, son of the **Hon. Colonel Braughton,** President of His Majesty's Council of this Province, is appointed Naval Officer of this Port in the Room of **M r. William Hammerton,** deceased.

The Ship *Fox* - **Captain Tolmas Arnold,** Commander.

Mr. Cobble writes the editor for a second time and shall be considered.

6 May 1732
Claret for sale, imported from Glasgow, at **Jacob Satur's** Store on the Bay.

All persons indebted to the **Hon. John Fenwick** arc hereby required to pay their debts. **Tho. Lamboll.**

Jesse Badenhop, Vendue Master.

All persons indebted to **Tho. Squire,** Vintner of Charlestown, are desired to pay same.

All persons indebted to the estate of **Richard Rowe,** deceased Vinter, late of Charlestown, are desired to pay the same to **John Moore** of Charlestown, administrator of the Estate. **Rowland Vaughn.**

Drifted from **Thomas Elliot's** new Bridge, a cypress canoe, 22' long belonging to **Thomas Smith** at Stono.

Jacob Woolford demands that all indebted to him clear their accounts.

Whereas on the 5th of May 1701, a tract of land containing 150 acres near Edisto was granted to **Richard Ireland** and then came into the hands of **Joseph Massey** and **Edward Small**, executors to **W. Windrass**, deceased. By **Thomas Ellery**.

Runaway from **Will. Webb** of Maggot's Island, but late of James Island, a Negro man named **Jackson Hercules**, and 2 Negro women named **Amoretta** and **Sarah**, being very clever Negroes. Reward offered for their return. Contact **M r s. Woodward** on James Island or **Mr. Thomas Bolton** of Charlestown.

13 May 1732

To be sold: the house on Church Street wherein **Mr. Evans**, the Taylor, now lives, consisting of nine rooms, eight of which have fire places. Also a kitchen and a storeroom. Contact **John Lloyd** at his plantation in Goose Creek or **John Balandine** in Charlestown.

John Lloyd will grant building leases of 64 acres of land, viz 8 lots of 8 acres each in the Parish of St. James on Goose Creek to encourage tradesmen to settle there. Land fronts the Broad Path, from the Brow of the hill **Mr. Rich Walker** now lives on to the fence joining **Mr. Hume's** land.

Reward offered for bay horse stolen or strayed from **Green**. Contact **Thomas Cooper** in Charlestown or **Mrs. Cross** at the Quarter House.

20 May 1732

Runaway: a Mustee wench about 18 years named **Phillis** and always brought up in Town, broke open her Master's box and took 110 pounds and other money. Contact **Samuel Smith** of Charlestown.

Yeoman and **Escott** - merchants.

On Thursday last, in Town, **Mr. Crawford** was married by **Mr. Basset** to **Miss Sally Bellamy**.

Mr. William Cattell, merchant of this town, was married in the Country by the **Rev. Mr. Guy** to **Miss Anne Cattell**, a relation to the said **Mr. Cattell**. Marriage on Wednesday last.

Cock fights to be held on the 9th instant at the house of Mr. S. Eldridge.

Runaway: a Mustee woman named **Diana** about 20 years of age formerly belonging to **Mrs. Mary Pike** at Goose Creek. Reward offered by her master **William Harvey** of Charlestown.

27 May 1732
Runaway: from **Daniel Cartwright**, Butcher, up the path, two Irish servant men, one a pretty husky fellow, with a blue coat, named **James Machone**, the other a short, well-set fellow, named **William Welsh**, a shoemaker by trade, who has taken some shoemaker's tools and a gun with him. A reward is offered.

Taken from **Mrs. Oliver's** house, a large pair of silver spurs and buckles. Reward offered.

Strayed out of **Mr. Saxby's** pasture up the path, two tame deer. Reward.

To be sold on June 5, at the plantation of **John Hill**, on the south side of Ashley River, near Jack's Savannah, 5 Negroes and other items.

To Be Sold by the Executrix of **William Hammerton**, deceased, land and two Negro children. Contact **Mrs. Hammerton**.

To Be Sold by public vendue on the 3rd of July, a plantation on Goose-Creek belonging to **Mr. Alexander Goodbee** bounding on land owned by **Tho. Clifford** and **James Goodbee**. Contact **John Daniel**.

A white horse, much flea-bitten about the head, stolen or strayed from Dorchester the 1st of March. Reward offered by **James Rousham** at Dorchester.

Stolen on the 23rd of May from the house of **John Bruce** in Charlestown an old Ebo Negro man, lately brought in by **Capt. Seaborn**.

10 June 1732
On June 9, the headmen of the Creek Indians now in town were entertained by **Mr. Eveleigh** at his house.

To Be Sold at the new store buildings on the Bay of Charlestown, the personal estate, including jewels and valuable collection of French books, of the late **Mr. Bernard Marett**, deceased, by **Jacob Woolford**.

Two lots to be sold in Treadd St. Inquire of **John Laurens**, sadler, in Charlestown.

17 June 1732

Runaway from **Stephen Ford** of John's Island, an Indian woman named **Sarah**, brought up to do housework, about 23 years old, speaks good English, has no marks on face. She had on a striped flannel gown. Deliver to **Stephen Ford** or **Thomas Fleming** in Charlestown.

Runaway from **James Searles**, one named **Delia** with a suckling child and the other named **Clarinda**. She formerly belonging to **Madam Trott**.

A Negro man named **Tony**, a bricklayer, formerly belonging to **Mr. Williams**, but now to **Hugh Hext**. Any person intending to employ this Negro must apply to **John Bee** in Charlestown who is impowered to receive his wages.

Runaway: a Negro boy named **Joe** from his master **Alexander Vanderdussen** formerly belonging to **Jacob Woolford**.

Auditor, **James St. John**, calls a meeting at his office next door to **Daniel Gibbon's** home in Charlestown.

24 June 1732

Mr. Goudet sworn as Collector and Naval Officer of Port Winyaw.

A violent storm of thunder and lightning did considerable damage to the house of **Dr. Thomas Smith** in Broad Street. It melted the blade of a sword in a scabbard and the muzzle of a gun, and flattened the whole house. Also damaged was **Captain Watkinson's** ship, the *King William*.

Died on Friday night, **Colonel Prioleau's** Indian, whose leg had been cut off because of a rattle snake bite.

A music recital is to be held for benefit of **Mr. Henry Campbell**.

House on Treadd St. joining Mr. Jeremiah Silver's. Inquire of **Thomas Lamboll** or **Michael James**, Glazier and Planter in Charlestown.

1 July 1732
James Abercomby – Attorney General of the Province **Charles Burley** – Register of the Court of Vice Admiralty.

8 July 1732
Died **Madam Johnson**, his Excellency the Governor's Lady, after a pretty long indisposition.

Wednesday last, two brothers of about 5 and 7 years of age, the sons of the late **widow Holson**, who is since married again, died suddenly, one in the morning, the other in the afternoon. Coroner's inquest determined that death of children was probably caused by excessive dose of some opiate. Further inquiry will be made.

A good store to be let, contact **Mr. Peach**, at the New Tavern in Church St.

Lost on Monday, fashionable Silver Salt with the letters NNH. Reward offered, **Nicholas Haimes**, Victualer in Charlestown.

Taken from **Mr. Stone's** house in Dorchester, a parcel of boots. Reward offered by **James Rouflarn**.

Anchovies sold by **Mrs. Bell**.

Stolen out of the lot of **Robert Hume** in Charlestown, a brown gelding belonging to **Thomas Ellery**. Reward.

15 July 1732
On the 29th past a white servant man belonging to **Mr. Robert Sinclair** wilfully drowned himself in Black River, he had been in the province but a few weeks, and is imagined that being put to work which he had not been used to, induced him to dispatch himself. He was found next day floating on the river, with half a score alligators about him that had made no scruples of working upon the poor fellow's carcass.

Monday morning last died **Eleazer Philips**, Planter here; as did the next day **Mr. Brown**, dancing master, at a Gentleman's Plantation in the Country, both after a very short illness. Others have died suddenly of Fevers in Town.

To Be Sold, the 19th instant by **Benjamin Godin** and **John Guerard**, a parcel of Gold Coast slaves imported from Barbados.

Whereas **James Smith** of Willtown, settled upon his wife, **Mary**, whose maiden name was **Mary Cochran**, after his decease an island opposite to Willtown, containing 160 acres and several lots of land in Willtown which he purchased of **Capt. William Scott** and sixteen named slaves. He appoints **William Livingston** and **James Cochran**, trustees. Notice given not to purchase any of this land from the said **James Smith** by **Benjamin Whitaker**, **Charles Pinckney**, **John Lewis**.

To Be Sold, good midding and brown bread by **Benjamin Haskins**, just arrived from Philadelphia at his home on the left hand side of **Thomas Elliott's** Bridge. The Brigt. *John*, **Benjamin Haskins**, will sail in a fortnight for Philadelphia.

All persons indebted to the late **Mr. Richard Edghill**, deceased are desired to pay his executor **Thomas Kimberly** in Charlestown.

5 August 1732

On the 24th of last month, was drowned in crossing over a creek near Cape Roman, **Mr. John Bampfield**, our Provost Marshal, with **Mr. Westlead** and four Negroes by the oversetting of their canoe. **Mr. Neal** is made Provost Marshal.

All persons indebted to the Estate of **Mr. William Brown**, Dancing Master are desired to pay **William Pinckney** and **William Kopes**, administrators at the house that **Mr. Richard Eagle** lived in which is to be let.

On Sunday last drowned **Mr. Morris Harvy**, the Pilot, oversetting his canoe. He was going ashore on Sullivan's Island.

On Tuesday last died **Mr. William Johnson**, his Excellency the Governor's second son.

Yesterday morning died **Mr. Henry Hargrave**, Deputy Secretary of this Province.

All persons that have any demands on or owe debts to the estate or **Mr. Joseph Hickins**, deceased, are desired to bring their accounts to Mesrs. **James Fowler** and **Joseph Miller**, executors.

14

12 August 1732

On Saturday last arrived here the ship *Prince William*, C a p t. P i c k, in about twelve weeks from London, by whom we hear that Capt. Dan. Bell belonging to this Place, and two of his men were washed overboard and drowned about a fortnight before the ship arrived in the River of Thames.

Chiefs of the Chickasaw Indians were met by his Excellency, they coming to pay compliments to his Excellency, at the Quarter House, they not being permitted to come any further because of illness in this town.

Strayed out of Col. Bull's pasture, near the Ferry, Mr. Secretary Hammerton's little dark bay horse bred in Mr. Domming's Pasture.

Strayed last Wednesday from Dr. Gibson's pasture, a grey coach horse branded with T. Elliott's mark. Also taken from the Doctor's stables a bay horse marked with Mrs. Monger's brand.

Thomas Russiat repeats that he is leaving the province and desires that those indebted to him, pay him.

T. Holton, Chairmaker on the Green.

19 August 1732

Mr. Alex Wood returning back from the Indian Country gives an account to his Excellency that on the Path in the Creek nation he found the body of Peter Shaw, Indian Trader, murdered and scalped, and his Servant ten yards away cruelly wounded.

The sickness which has afflicted this town is (by the blessing of God) now almost over.

Good Cocao sold by John Dart in Charlestown.

To Be Sold a very good Negro House Wench with two children. Treat with Mrs. Martha Romsey in Charlestown.

Joseph Morgan at the Beer Cellar against Mr. Elliott's B r i d g e on the Bay, continues to sell beer as usual, and carries on the brewing, at his late father's house on the Green.

Cabinet work sold at New-Market Plantation, a mile from town by Broomhead and Blythe. Other items also sold.

26 August 1732

St. Andrews Club to meet on the 30th of Nov. at the House of Mr. **Henry Gignilliat** in Charlestown. By order of the Honorable **Alexander Skene**, President. **Walter Brown**, Clerk.

Runaway from **Abraham Sutar**, at Black River, a black well-set Negro man called **Caffe** with a cut on his shoulder and one of his arms, being a Gold Coast Negro. Contact **Jacob Sutar** in Charlestown.

Dying done by Mr. **Bartram**.

All persons having demands on the Estate of **George Rolfe**, deceased are desired to present them to **Samuel Eveleigh**, adm. To Be Sold by public vendue, under the New Market House, a choice collection of valuable books in Law, Physick and Divinity.

All persons indebted to the Estate of Mr. **James LeChautre**, deceased are desired to pay the same to **Mr. William Yeomans** and Mr. **John Guernier**.

Whereas **Capt. Richard Harris**, late of Berkley County Planter, did on the 3rd day of February, 1731, execute his last will in the presence of **George Logan**, **Henry Bossard**, and **Issac Lesene, Jr.**; thereby did bequeath the sum of 100 pounds to the Minister of the Parish of St. Thomas for the maintenance and education of the poor children of the said Parish, and did give to his wife, **Hannah Harris**, seven Negroes and half the yearly profits of his estate for her life, and after several other small legacies, did give to **Elizabeth Baker**, his wife Hannah's grandaughter, the remainder of the Estate, of very great value. **John Daniel** was constituted sole executor and guardian of her estate, and whereas the said **Hannah Harris**, on about the 16th day of August, in order to defeat the execution of the pious intentions of the said **Richard Harris**, having received from **John Daniel** the right to pursue the will, did tear the same to pieces, and has since sold and made away with a great part of the stock of cattle and personal items of **Richard Harris**. All are forbidden to buy or receive from **Hannah Harris** any of the estate, there being a suit filed in the Court of Chancery against the said **Hannah Harris** to establish the said will by **Benjamin Whitaker** and **Charles Pinckney**.

2 September 1732

To be let or sold, the house belonging to **Capt. Bee** in Church St. with a good store adjoining.

Mrs. Mary Harvey in Charlestown has two rooms to let, both with fireplaces.

To Be Sold by **Mrs. Peach**, at the New Tavern in Church Street, a choice collection of pictures by the best hands.

All persons indebted to **Mr. David Davies**, Currier, deceased, are desired to pay the same to **Albert Detmar**, adm.

9 September 1732

To Be Sold by **Issac Chardon**, good cloths.

John King sells sugar, tea, soaps, linens, etc.

Taken up at Savannah (by a Negro fellow of **Capt. Thomas Johnson's**), a Negro man of about 40 years branded on the left breast with a figure of 9 and says he belongs to **Mr. McTear** of Pond Pond.

To Be Sold: **Mr. John Moore**, all his messuages and tenements on both sides of **Mr. Trott's** great house in Charlestown.

16 September 1732

Lately found a bond, upon Ashley Ferry Road, from **Ebenezer Singleton** to **John Oldfield** and **Wm. Adams** for 200 pounds and on the back of said bond, an endorsement by **John Oldfield** to **Samuel Rigg**.

All persons indebted to the estate of **Mr. Mungo Welsh**, deceased are desired to pay the same to **James Crokatt**, adminstrator.

To Be Sold, 1/2 a lot with 2 houses on it upon the Green in Charlestown belonging to **Mr. Edgar Wells**, **Samuel Shaddock** now living in it.

All persons having any demands on or indebted to the Estate of **George Bampfield**, late Provost Marshal, deceased are desired to bring their accounts to **Mrs. Elizabeth Bampfield**, administratrix.

All persons having any demands on or indebted to the Estate of **Col. Alexander Trench**, deceased, are desired to bring their accounts to Mesrs. **Ribton Hutchinson** and **Richard Woodward**, Adms.

Runaway Negro slave called **Sambo**, nicknamed "the Lawyer", who formerly belonged to Mrs. **Montjay**. Contact **Ribton Hutchinson**.

23 September 1732

To be let, rent free for seven years, only repairing the house and land at Red Bank where Mesrs. **Tradd, Dry** and **Pickering** and afterwards Mesrs. **Nisbett** and **Kinloch** kept store. Contact **Jacob Motte** in Charlestown.

A choice young parcel of slaves to be sold at the house of Mr. **Child** at Strawberry Ferry. **James LeBas.**

To Be Sold by **John** and **Alexander Rigg**, a complete set of tools.

Word received from Savannah is that all Indian Traders are safe and that the Creek Indians were concerned at the death of **Peter Shaw** and his man and have reason to believe it must have been done by some Cherokees and that a body of them were preparing to go to war against the Creeks and that another body of them was going to Flint River to take up his horses and goods and carry them to Ochyes, the town to which he was bound.

30 September 1732

A concert of vocal and instrumental music to be held on Oct. 6 at the Council Chamber. Tickets can be had at Mrs. **Cook's** and at Mrs. **Saureau's** house.

Jenys and Baker, merchants.

Runaway from his **Excellency Robert Johnson, Esq.**, a white servant man, named **John Saxon**, a Stone Cutter by trade, about 32 years of age. He is a middle-sized man with reddish hair and beard, and broke out in his face. Reward offered.

Imported on the Schooner *Elizabeth and Mary* from London, a choice parcel of men and women servants, most of them trades. Agree with the Master **James Wilks** at Mr. **William Pinckney's** on the Bay.

To Be Sold on October 5 by **George Austin** a choice parcel of Negroes imported on the Ship *Edward* to be seen on the ship at Eliott's Wharf.

To Be Sold by **George Logan,** a plantation containing 620 acres of land, etc., situated on Wandoo River about 12 miles from Charlestown.

A tract of land containing 150 acres about 2 miles up Quelch's Creek in Christ Church Parish, etc. Contact **John White** of the same parish. Rice on land to be sold.

Two barrels brought over by **Capt. Pick** and at **Capt. Proctor's** store, one marked TC Store and the other PW Store, need to be claimed.

7 October 1732
Runaway: a Boussue Negro man named **Aaron** who used to go about town with a cart and a mule. Reward offered by master **Daniel Bourget.**

To Be Sold by **Thomas Smith,** 7000 acres of land on Charlestown Neck from 10 to 35 miles from town. Contact at his plantation on Goose Creek about 11 miles from Charlestown.

All persons having demands on estate of **Dr. William Napier,** deceased, are ordered to deliver them to **John Lewis** in Charlestown. All indebted to estate are to pay **James Bullock** in Willtown, executor of the deceased's last will, or to **Mr. Lewis** in Charlestown.

All persons indebted to **Alexander Smith,** Taylor, are desired to pay same by the 11th of January next for **Smith** intends to leave the province.

All persons to whom the estate of **John Arnolt,** deceased, is indebted are desired to bring in their accounts and those who owe estate are notified to pay same. **Charles Pinckney.**

John Grove offer⸱ ᶠnr sale, ten choice Negroes imported in the Ship *Edward* to ʰ ᴉⁿ ᵃt **Edward Steed's** plantation, known by the name Newₘ.⸱ket Plantation.

14 October 1732
On Thursday last, one **Thomas Morrison,** being disordered in his senses, drowned himself.

To Be Sold in Dorchester town at the house of **Mr. McColume** lately deceased, two Negroes, cattle, etc. By **Malachi Glaze.**

Strayed from Charlestown about 10 months ago, a small bay horse, with a star on his forehead and a switch tail, branded RM. Reward offered by **John Frazier** of Charlestown.

All persons who have any demands on **Captain John Gascoigne** of the Ship *Alborough* are desired to present them.

A house in Broad Street opposite to **M r . H u m e ' s** to be let. Also a tenement in Tradd Street. Inquire of **Robert Johnston** or **Edward Holland.**

To Be Sold: a tract of land on the Pon Pon River about 1 1/2 miles from the Pon Pon Ferry, a mile from **Mesrs. Mathews** and **Randal's** Store containing 400 acres of rice land and 200 acres of cypress swamp. May be purchased from **William Levingston** at Willtown, and information from **John Colcock** in Charlestown.

Drugs sold by **Samuel Everleigh.**

Whereas **John Moore** of Charlestown swears that in May last, he saw, in the hands of **Capt. Richard Harris** of Berkley County, a bond for £500 due to **Harris** from **Mrs. Martha Logan**, mother of **John Daniel** of this county, on which bond **Mr. Harris** indorsed to the Vestry of St. Thomas Parish as an addition to **Mr. Beresford's** donation for the use of a Charity School in the said Parish and the said **Mr. Daniel** having immediately possessed himself of all papers and money of the said **Harris** upon his decease, the said bond not yet paid to the Vestry, I thought it necessary to advertise, lest the bond be stifled and the Charity defeated. **Hannah Harris.**

21 October 1732
Died suddenly on Saturday night, a servant woman belonging to **Mr. Gates** of this Place.

For the benefit of **Mr. Saltor** at the Council Chamber on the 25th, a concert of music with a BALL following. Tickets to be had at **Mrs. Saureau's.**

Mary Beckman of St. Paul's Parish in Colleton County, has eloped from her husband and he is no longer responsible for her debts. **Titus Beckman.**

Plantation five miles of Charlestown with orchard of good fruit trees, etc., to be sold or let by **James Crokatt**. Also Madeira wine, bottled red port and French claret.

All persons who have demands on the Estate of **Dr. John Monteith**, deceased, are notified to present them to **James Greme** of Charlestown. All persons indebted to the estate or to **Dr. Thomas Cooper** in Company with the deceased are desired to pay them to **James Greme**.

Alexander Parris, Comissary, gives notice that he wants 200 Barrels of Beef for the public service. Also threatens prosecution of those carrying away mud and oyster shells from the Marsh lying opposite Charlestown, it being his land.

To Be Sold Lot 23 at Georgetown, Winyaw, fronting the Bay. Contact **Mr. Elias Horry** at Santee or **Wm. Romsey** in Charlestown.

Notice to all persons who had work done by **Charles Holyday**, deceased, for the past two years and are indebted to him, shall pay **Major Hugh Butler**, one of his executors, at his plantation.

A plantation containing 400 acres bounding on the north side of Wando River about 18 miles from Charlestown for sale. Inquire of **Jeremiah Roper**, the possessor thereof.

28 October 1732

On Sunday there were near 200 Negroes on the Green and one having drank too much, drew out a knife and stuck a valuable Negro, belonging to **Mrs. Elliot**, in the neck, so that his life is in danger.

A fine appearance of good company was present for the concert for the benefit of **Mr. Salter**. A ball afterwards was opened by the **Lord Forester** and **Miss Hill**.

All persons indebted to **Mr. Thomas Snow**, deceased are obliged to pay **Richard Hill**, adm. of his estate. By **Benjamin Whitaker**.

To Be Sold: a plantation containing 300 acres with 10 slaves etc., on the south side of the Ashley River, about 5 miles from Charlestown. Inquire of **Charles Hill**, Charlestown, merchant.

Strayed from the Green, two horses formerly belonging to Mr. Hill Cross at the Quarter House. Reward offered by Daniel Welshuyssin.

Linens for sale by Francis le Brasseur at his house near Capt. Anson's.

Ribton Hutchinson, merchant, near the Bay offers for sale china, hats, silver, etc.

Runaway from his Master's Plantation in the Parish of St. James Goose-Creek, a lusty Negro man named Hercules. He formerly used to wait on his Master in Charlestown and is now by trade a Cooper. Reward offered by his master Robert Hume on Charlestown Neck.

Runaway from Pond Pond, an Indian wench named Deborah, age 22, speaks good English, and is very handy at women's work. Has a sore above her heels, her fore teeth out and her great toes point inward. Reward offered for her return to her master, Joseph Didcott, at Pond Pond Ferry.

A complete wheel plough lately bought in England for sale. Inquire of Nicholas Haines in Charlestown.

4 November 1732
All persons having demands on Captain James Lloyd, Commander of the *Happy*, are desired to bring them in so they may paid.

Negro wench, age 18, to be sold by Jacob Motte of Charlestown.

Runaway from his Master, John Richards, a Perriauver Man belonging to Winyaw on the 29th of Oct., a white servant man named Philip Jones, a barber by trade, 19 years old, of a fresh complexion and fair hair. Had on when he left, a brown double-breasted pea jacket, a pair of sail cloth trousers, blue stockings and new shoes. Please bring to James Fowler of Charlestown, or the town prison. Reward offered by John Richards.

Dr. Varambaut, lately come into this Province, advertises his cures and fees. His lives at Mrs. Dupoisdon's in Charlestown.

Runaway from the Plantation formerly belonging to **Capt. Douglas**, near Dorchester, a tall thin Negro fellow named **Tower-Hill** and talks bad English. Bring to **John Watter** at **Mr. Alex. Skene, Jr.**, or to **Mrs. Pickering** in Charlestown for a reward.

Edward Simpson, merchant at Ashley Ferry.

11 November 1732

Major **James Richards** is appointed Major and Capt. of the Company of Switzers lately arrived here.

A proclamation was published forbidding **James St. John** surveyor or any of his deputies to run out on his Excellency's lands.

Joseph Fox, clerk in absence of **Mr. Badenhop**.

Lost on Weds. night between **Mr. Gignilliot's** and **Mrs. Surrow's** about 11:00 a Red Turkey Leather Pocket Book with Constantinople gilt on it with £200 in it. Reward offered by **Mr. Jacob Satur** on the Bay.

To Be Sold, a plantation called Blessing containing 1000 acres joining Cooper River. Inquire of **Peter Robert**.

Four choice young Negro fellows to be sold by **James Kilpatrick**.

Absented herself from on board the *Eliz & Mary* Schooner, **James Wilks**, Commander, a white servant woman named **Mary Worrel**. Reward offered by **William Pinckney**.

Plantation to be sold on the South side of Ashley River, about four miles from Charlestown, containing 300 acres of land. Inquire of **William Cattell** or **Benjamin Godfrey**, who live on the plantation.

18 November 1732

Runaway from **Capt. James Lloyd**, Commander of his Majesty's Snow *Happy*, two boys, one named **John Cameron**, of a freckled face, short sandy hair, and well fed; the other named **John Tanner**, a pale face boy with lank hair, having both of them blue dussil jackets, and much of a height. Reward offered bring to **Capt. Griffin**, Commander of the *Shoreham*.

All persons indebted to, or having demands on **Levi Durand** are desired to settle them. He intends to leave for Great Britain directly.

Runaway a Negro woman named **Incky**, who formerly belonged to **Henry Gibbes**. Bring to **James Fisher** on the Bay for reward.

All persons having demands on estate of the late **John Buchanan**, deceased are desired to deliver them to **William Cattell, Jr.**, in Charlestown. All persons indebted to the estate are to pay debts to either **William Levingston** in Willtown, executor of the deceased's last will, or to **William Cattell, Jr.**

To Be Sold in St. John's Parish, 500 acres with house and 220 head of cattle, etc. Inquire of **Joseph Mackey** at Pond Pond, or **John Bayly** at Goose Creek.

To Be Sold a plantation containing 46 acres (near the Quarter House and about 5 miles from Charlestown). Treat with **Tho. Ellery** in Charlestown or with **Benjamin Dennis**.

25 November 1732
Goods to be sold at **Mr. Daniel Townsends** near Elliott's Bridge.

Stolen out of the stable behind the Church in Charlestown, now in possession of **Mr. Neal** the Provost Marshall, a dark brown Virginia bred gelding. Bring to **Rowland Vaughan** in Charlestown for reward. Horse had previously been advertised in paper by **Thomas Ellery**.

Strayed, two white geldings belonging to **Childermas Croft**, next door to **Dr. Gibson's** in Charlestown.

At **Dan. Bourget's**, Brewer, in old Church St. behind the old Church-Yard is good stabling and entertainment for horses.

Good fresh currants sold by **Henry Bedon**.

2 December 1732
From the Indian country we hear that on the 2nd of September, there fell a great shower of hail, at a town called Tessakey. Hail stones as large as Pullet's egg came into **Mr. Locklin McBean's** store.

All persons indebted to the estate of Mr. William Chetham deceased, are desired to pay Mr. Edward Simpson at Ashley Ferry or Mr. John Champneys in Charlestown.

A fine young Negro man, who has had the small pox, brought up in the carpenter's trade, and a very good spinett, to be sold by Eliz. Bampfield.

To Be Sold a choice parcel of plantation slaves, to be let a parcel of convenient store houses in the Governor's Alley. Inquire of Tweedie Somerville.

9 December 1732
A list of European goods for sale by John Jones, at the Widow Romsey's on the Bay.

Meeting of St. Andrew's Club, on St. Andrew's Day, the 30th of Nov. at the house of Henry Gignilliat where a handsome entertainment of about 40 dishes was provided for supper. Present were Gov. Robert Wright, Chief Justice Capt. James Lloyd, Alex. Skene, Eleazer Allen, Wm. Saxby and forty other members residing in the province. New members admitted were Capt. Tho. Griffen, Commander of the Ship the Shoreham, James Douglas, Lt. of the same ship, Dan Welshyuson, The Rev. Mr. Edw. Dyson, A.M., The Rev. Mr. Archb. Stobo, The Rev. Mr. John Wetherspoon, Dr. Rob. Smith, Mr. Wm. Stobo, Mr. Wm. Swinton, and Mr. James Michie. Officers for the year coming were chosen - Alexander Skene, President, John Fraser, Vice-President, James Crokatt, Treasurer, James Greme, Assistant, James Michie, Secretary.

On Sunday last died a sailor, belonging to a Sloop recently arrived from the Barbados. Said to have been unmercifully beaten by his Captain who was imprisoned.

Died suddenly of an appolexy on Monday last, within sight of his plantation at Goose Creek, Mr. Jacob Satur, a wealthy merchant of this town.

A likely Negro fellow to be sold, has had the small pox, a ship carpenter and wheelwright by trade. Inquire of Anne Lovey.

Samuel Vincent intends to depart this province in eight to ten days and desires to settle his accounts.

All persons indebted to **Edward Hext** are desired to pay the same to **John Bee** in Charlestown. Notice by **Tho. Ellery**.

Whereas several persons have been indebted to **Adam Battin** for schooling, writing, etc., are desired to pay by Jan. 1st.

All persons indebted to **James Crokatt**, Merchant are desired to pay same or they will be sued by **James Greme**.

To Be Sold two tracts of land near Dorchester town. One tract containing 140 acres the other 103 acres both with several houses. Also 1 lot fronting the river in Dorchester with a good new birch dwelling house. Inquire of **Gilison Clapp** in Charlestown.

A good Chariot-Berlin with the harness to be sold by **Issac Mazyck, Sr.**

To be let a plantation containing upwards of 100 acres, within 1 1/2 miles of Charlestown with a good dwelling house. Treat with **Thomas Godsen**.

John Purkis, Smith, of London now lives in Tread Street in Charlestown and supplies Smith's work.

16 December 1732
Choice parcel of good blue and white cottons for sale by **Joseph Skute**.

James Walker, Peruke Maker of Charlestown, plans to leave this province soon and desires his accounts to be settled. By **James Greme**.

Runaway from **Johnathan Main**, a Negro man named **Mingo**, lame of one leg, a shoemaker by trade.

Lately imported to be sold by **Issac Chardon**, striped flannels, blue cottons, bed blankets, etc.

Dropped at the house of **Mr. Gignilleat** on the 15th at night, a Buff Sword Belt with a large silver clasp and buttons. T. **Neophilus Gregory** offers reward for its return.

Runaway from **Thomas Stitsmith's** house in Broad St., a young Negro fellow named **Harry** who used to attend **Dr. Gibson's** shop on the Bay.

Whereas the last will and testament of Col. Alexander Trench, deceased, has been lately proved; whereby Benjamin Whitaker, the surviving executor therein named, the same undertakes to settle the deceased's accounts.

To Be Sold by Benjamin Godin and John Guerard, a parcel of Negroes, imported directly from Gambia, in the Ship *Molley Galley*, Capt. John Carruthers.

John Hamerton, His Majesty's Receiver General, announces that he has received orders to distrain upon every person that has not paid His Majesty's Quit Rent.

23 December 1732

Two new members of the Commons House of Assembly are to be elected in room of William Donning and Alexander Trench, deceased.

His Excellency Robert Johnson, Gov. offers reward for arrest of John Connette, Drummer, John Pemble, Mathew Hicks, and Will Thompson, all soldiers belonging to Capt. Edward Massey's Independent Co. who have lately deserted. Description:

John Pemble - aged 25 years and 5'8", well set, pretty fresh coloured in the face, thick spoken, and short black hair.

John Connette - aged 23 years and 5'5", fair faced, slow spoken, his knees inclining something to one another, and short footed.

William Thompson - a short thick squat fellow, a brown complexion, with short black hair, not free in discourse, but of a smiling countenance.

Mathew Hicks - a tall slender fellow 26 years of age with sandy colored hair, very brisk and free in discourse, but of an indifferent countenance.

Mr. Benjamin Godin, agent of Capt. Edward Massey will see that the 1.5 is paid upon their delivery.

All persons indebted to Hugh Evans, Taylor, are desired to pay. Notice by Rowland Vaughns.

All persons indebted to the estate of Mr. Jacob Satur, Merchant late of Charlestown, deceased, are desired to pay Mrs. James Ollier, adm. of said estate as she intends to depart the province as soon as possible.

27

Sarah Smith, wife of Mikell Smith, deceased, gives notice that she will not administer her husband's estate.

Stolen or strayed, a dark bay gelding out of the yard of Mr. Wm. Gibbes, on the Green. Whoever returns the said gelding to Mr. Gibbes or the owner Tho. Barlow at Wappoo will be rewarded.

Runaway: about three months ago, a man servant, belonging to Col. Peter Purry, named John Peter Bovet, born at Neuschatel, a carpenter, about 23 years of age, of a middle size, full of face but pale and poxpitted with sore eyes, wearing a wig and a cinnamoned colored coat. Bring him to Mr. Issac Chardon, Merchant, in Charlestown for a reward.

30 December 1732

Last week, we had advice from Alex. Wood, from the Upper Creeks, that Simon Leach, his license man, Robert Johnson, ---- Lewis, together with a half breed brother to James Welsh, deceased, were found dead, about half way in the Path, between the Cousa's and Chickasaw's with their heads cut off, and their horses and goods carried away; it is supposed to be done by the Choctaws at the instigation of the French.

On Wednesday last Col. John Peter Purry, let out, in three Pettiangers, with 87 Switzers, in order to settle a colony on Savannah River, in Granville County and was saluted with seven guns from the bastion at their parting.

The Governor appointed Joseph Edward Flowers to be Captain and John Savy to be Lt. under Col. Purry.

All persons indebted to David Allan, Vintner, of Charlestown, are desired to pay same by the first of February as David Allan intends to depart the province. Rowland Vaughns.

John King, merchant.

Justinus Stoll, Blacksmith, next to Granvile's Bastion on the Bay.

All persons indebted to Sam. Eveleigh, Merchant, are desired to pay same before the 1st of Jan. or be sued by Robert Hume.

Large bay black horse strayed from Mrs. Eliz. Weatherick's on the north side of Ashley River. Whoever returns the horse to Mrs. Elizabeth Weatherick or Sarah Screven on James's Island will be rewarded.

Lost from White Point in Charlestown, a Pettianger that carries about 30 barrels of rice. Reward offered by Sarah Screven.

To be let, the house Mr. Basset lives in, with a large garden and out buildings. Inquire of Joseph Moody.

NEWSPAPER ABSTRACTS - 1733

6 January 1733

On Tuesday last, the Troop of Horse Guards, commanded by **Col. Samuel Prioleau**, was exercised on the Green. After which several communications were read appointing **John Smith**, Major, **Wm. Fuller**, Captain, **Rene Ravenel**, Lieut., **John Fairchild**, Cornet, **Thomas Totnel**, Quarter Master, and **Thomas Fairchild**, Field Marshall of the said troop.

A. Garden writes the editor objecting to his refusing to publish submitted items.

Thomas Trowell, at the house **Mrs. Hayden** lived in, next door to **Mr. John Shepherd's** in Elliot's St. desires to sell European goods immediately as he intends to return to Great Britain.

Good salt and pistol gunpowder sold by **Thomas Bolton** on the Bay.

Runaway from **Mrs. Gale's** Plantation, about 2 miles from Charlestown, a Mullatto fellow named **James**.

Jonas Spoke, living at **Mr. Aigron**, Silversmith, near the French Church, makes beds and mattresses.

Whereas **Henry Chidley, Abraham Duboit & Edward Gilbert**, were committed to the custody of the Provost Marshall for several felonies, which persons in the Night between the 4th and 5th broke the jail and escaped. Reward offered by **James Neale**, Prov. Marshal.

Runaway from **John Thompson, Jun.** a white servant man, named **Peter Robertson** on Dec. 5 past, he's a short fellow, with short brown hair, somewhat pockfretten. Had on a narrow brimmed hat, a light colored pea jack of kersey cloth, a pair of ozenbrig trousers, and a pair of white negro cloth breeches, he's bandy leg'd, and commonly walks stooping, and pretends to be somewhat of a cooper. Reward offered by master **John Thompson, Jun.**

Whereas Mess. **Gibson** and **Stitsmith's** partnership is ending and **Stitsmith** intends to discontinue practicing in Charlestown, All persons indebted to them for Physick and Surgery are desired to pay by Feb. 10. **Ths. Stitsmith, Daniel Gibson.**

Stolen or strayed from **Arthur Middleton,** at his plantation at Goose Creek, a grey gelding. Bring horse to **Arthur Middleton** at Goose Creek or **John Braileford** at Mr. **Wragg's** in Charlestown for reward, no questions asked.

Gabriel Laban at Stone Landing near _____ **Colleton's, Esq.** has opened a store where he sells goods and strong liquors.

Whoever has title or claim to any of the hereafter described lands, may be informed how to come by their Grants of the same, by the Printer.

July 14, 1696 – A grant to **Philip Rowland** of 100 acres in Berkley County at Wampee Swamp, butting to the northward on **Lambert Saunders,** westward on **Thomas Williams,** eastward on **James Jones** and **Christopher Walker,** southward on Walker.

Jan. 2, 1697 – A grant to **John Hamilton** of 80 acres in Colleton Co. lying on Edisto Island, to the northwest on **Christooher Linkley,** etc.

Sept. 1, 1697 – A grant to **James Dumabe** of 100 acres in Berkley Co. on the north side of the Ashby River to the southward by the said **Dumabe** and **James Plock,** westward on **Tho. Butler,** eastward **Plock.**

May 1699 – A grant to **Christopher Jarrard** of 100 acres in Berkley Co. on the northernmost side of Newtown Creek, south westward on **T. Drayton,** north westward on **David Davis,** north eastward on **Allen.**

1702 – A grant to **Garrat Dillion** of 200 acres of land in Colleton Co. on the north side of Combee River, bounding to the northeast on **John Palmer,** to the southeast on **John Seabrook,** to the southwest on Combee River, and to the northwest on **William Page.**

1709 – A grant to **Wm. Pool** of 60 acres in Berkley Co. lying on Wisburo Creek, to the southwest on **Pool's** land to the southeast on **Charles Hayes.**

1709 – A grant to **Henry Brunneau** of 500 acres in Craven

Co. butting to the south on the Santee River, to the east on **Pet. Guillaird.**

1709 – A grant to **Daniel Brebant** of 26 acres in Berkley Co. to the northeast on Wisburo Creek, to the southeast on **Videau's** land, to the northwest on **Charles Hays.**

Oct. 6, 1709 – A grant to **John Gough** of 563 acres of cedar swamp on the head of the eastern branch of Cooper River.

13 January 1733

Peter Horry, merchant in Mr. Wragg's Alley advertises large amount of goods for sale.

Good Old England Soal Leather sold by **Jonathain Main** on the Bay.

All persons having demands on the estate of **Mr. Benjamin Massey,** deceased are desired to bring their accounts to **John Bee, Jr.** and **James Mathews,** his executors in Charlestown. Those who left any guns or other works in the deceased's hands are desired to send to his widow on the Green to receive these items.

All persons indebted to **Mrs. Charlotte Gouiran** are desired to pay the same.

To be sold by **Charles Lownds,** in Charlestown, by public vendue, a choice parcel of Negroes, etc.

Runaway from his Master, **Nathanial Ford,** at Hobkoy a Negro man named **Primus** formerly belonging to **Landgrave Smith** and **Mr. Binford,** merchants in Charlestown.

To be sold on the 15th a parcel of house and plantation slaves, lately belonging to **Col. Alexander Trench,** deceased by **Richard Wigg,** D.V.M. **Benjamin Whitaker,** executor of estate.

All persons who have any demands on the estate of **John Coleman,** late of Savannah Town, deceased are desired to bring accounts to **Jordan Roche,** Adm. (he designing to leave the province soon) or to **William Cattell, Jun.**

Whereas **Mrs. Sarah Ward** intends to depart the province soon, she desires to have accounts settled. Notice by **Charles Pinckney.**

Runaway from **Stephen Russel** on James Island, an apprentice named **John Nathan**, had on a blue coat, and a long pale Ozenbrig Breeches. Reward.

All persons indebted to **Elezar Phillips** and his son, deceased are desired to pay him, or **Benjamin Savage**, merchant. He intending to leave the province the beginning of next month.

20 January 1733

On Saturday night came to anchor in our town a ship with about 120 people for settling the new colony of Georgia in which was **James Oglethorp** who came ashore that night and was well received by the Governor. The next morning the ship sailed for Port Royal.

Smallpox hits two families in Winyaw.

Buried in Charlestown the week pass - 7, baptized - 1.

European goods for sale at the house **Mrs. Haydon** lived in on Elliot's Street.

To be sold a parcel of young Negro men lately imported by **Capt. Stephen Haven**. Treat with the said Capt. on his ship at Elliott's wharf or at **James Fisher's** near the wharf.

Choice cargo of European goods including wigs and Madeira wine imported by **Capt. Lee** from London and sold by **James Crokatt**.

Runaway from Goose-Creek Point, a tall elderly Spanish Negro man named **J o h n**. Reward offered by his master **Alexander Vanderdussen**.

Richard Eagles of Charlestown desires to depart this province in a short time and wishes to settle accounts. By **C h a r l e s Pinckney**.

European goods sold by **Wm. Lasserre** at his store at **Mr. Lloyd's** on the Bay.

All persons indebted to **Wm. Linthwaite**, shopkeeper of Charlestown are desired to pay their debts by March 25 so he can pay his creditors. By **Charles Pinckney**.

To be let by **Capt. Thomas Heyward** on James Island, a large garden with several fine orange trees, etc. Inquire of Hayward or of **John Laurens**, sadler in Charlestown to whom all persons who have any accounts with **Mrs. Eliz. Stephens**, Deceased, are desired to apply.

All persons having any accounts upon the estate of **Joseph Miller**, Taylor on his own or in company with **Alexander Smith** are desired to bring accounts to his executors the said **Alexander Smith** and **Adam Bantin**.

All persons are forewarned not to employ two Negro carpenters by name of **Mingo** and **Norwich** belonging to **Lawrence Dennis** of Charlestown without first dealing with **Dennis** or his spouse.

J. Lambert from England opens a store at **Wm. Pinckney's** on the Bay.

Whereas I have purchased a servant who is a chimney sweeper intending thereby to prevent the danger that threatens this town from chimneys and many complaints being made to me that the chimney keeper often neglects to sweep their chimneys. Therefore to prevent complaints, I give notice to all persons to deal with me for his services as long as he is a servant to **Daniel Green**. Whereas I intend to depart this province soon for health reasons all persons indebted to me are desired to pay same by March 25 or be sued by **Benjamin Whitaker**.

27 January 1733

On Saturday last, a Negro fellow belonging to **Issac Mazyck**, senior, pulled a young lad off his horse, on the Broad Path, and rode away with his horse and bags thereon. He was taken on Sunday, on Monday brought to town, tried and condemned and the next day, about noon, he was hanged.

Buried in Charlestown this pass week – 6, Baptized – 2.

Thomas Trowell, who plans to leave this province in 20 days, sells goods at the house **Mrs. Haydon** lived in on Elliott Street.

Samuel Eveleigh, merchant.

All persons having demands on the estate of Michael Mac-namara are notified that his wife, Mrs. Christian Mac-namara will not administer his estate.

At the Council-Chamber on the 5th of February will be a con-sort of vocal and instrumental music. Tickets to be had at Mrs. Cooks and at Mrs. Saurreau's House.

To be let a plantation on James Island by Daniel Gibson, Sur-geon in Charlestown.

Whereas George Hall of Wattboo, Storekeeper desires to depart this province on the 25th of March he asks that his ac-counts be settled. By Thomas Ellery.

To be sold on the head of the middle branch of the Stono River 432 acres. Inquire of Capt. John Jenkins, living in Charles-town.

3 February 1733

On Sunday last arrived here, the Ship *King William*, William Watkinson, Commander in about ten weeks from London, in whom arrived Morley, who has patents for being Provost Mar-shall, Clerk of the Crown and Clerk of the Peace.

On the 21st of last month, a Negro man belonging to John Carmichael at Spoon's Savannah was found dead, with 10 Swan shot in his head about 3 or 400 yards from his house. Reward offered by his master for information concerning his death.

James McClellan, cabinet maker, from London living next door to Joseph Massey in Church Street advertises his serv-ices.

All persons indebted to Joseph Law deceased, are desired to pay their debts to John Vandrolarst or Thomas Barksdale, executors.

All persons having demands on the estate of James LeChantre late of Charlestown, Shopkeeper, deceased are desired to bring in their accounts to Mess. William Yeomans and John Garnier. By Charles Pinckney.

A tract of 400 acres of land, lying six miles from Stono Land-ing to be let by Mrs. Anne Drayton.

10 February 1733

Francis le Brasseur has opened a store where Mr. **Rigg** lived in Elliot Street.

A lot to be sold in Beaufort Town, #64 bounding to the East on West Street. Inquire of **Mr. Davis** at **Col. Parris's**.

Good salt to be sold by **Henry** and **Alexander Percuneau**.

To be sold a plantation containing 1000 acres, 700 of which is rice land, with a large garden, etc. Inquire of **John Laurens**, Sadler in Charlestown.

All persons indebted to **Daniel Greene**, Merchant in Charlestown, are desired to pay the same by the 25th of March next or they will be sued. He desiring to depart this province, in a short time for the recovery of his health.

All persons indebted to the **Hon. John Feniwicke** and Co., upon bond, are desired off the interest due in March next at the house of **Tho. Lloyd** in Charlestown. By **Thomas Lamboll**.

17 February 1733

Delivered by mistake from on Board the *Abigal and Anne* a box containing two dozen laced hats and wigs. If you have received these goods send them to **Capt. Tho. Henning** or **James Crokatt**.

Stolen or strayed out of **Mrs. Oliver's** Stables in Broad St. a Roan mare. Reward offered by **Mr. Brande** in Charlestown.

Jacob Motte on the Bay advertises two lots for sale in Charlestown.

Negroes, horses, cattle, sheep, hogs, etc. to be sold by **Mrs. Sarah Scriven** at her house on James Island.

Lost, the beginning of this month, a gold girdle buckle. Bring to **Joseph Massy** in Charlestown or to **George Oliver** on Wando Neck for reward.

To be sold by **John Farr**, 300 acres about a mile and a half from Stono Bridge, 30 acres cleared.

Goods to be sold by **John** and **Alexander Rigg** at **Mrs. Ramsey's** on the Bay.

Negro man named **Peter** to be sold by **John Simmons**, he's a bricklayer, plasterer and white washer. Inquire at **Capt. Scot's** on the Bay.

To be sold on the 22nd of March, a plantation within a mile of Dorchester town belonging to **Col. Glover's** Estate containing 600 acres of land, with a beautiful dwelling house, 45' long, 35' wide, 2 floors, 4 rooms on a floor with buffets, closets, etc. and a dry cellar underneath with several and convenient rooms. Also 1000 acres over Pond Pond River about 4 miles from **Mr. Parker's** ferry. By **Malachia Glaze** and **Lawrence Sanders**.

24 February 1733
The ship *Rebecca*, **John Cornuck**, Master will sail in 8 or 10 days. For freight or passage, agree with **Samuel Eveleigh**, merchant.

Whereas it was lately advertised that all persons indebted to the estate of **Joseph Miller**, deceased are to pay debts to executors, **Alex. Smith** and **Alan Battin** who have impowered **Robert Roper** to receive these sums but there has been small regard to this notice. Compliance is hereby commanded or suit will be filed by **James Greeme**.

Two lots in Charlestown to be sold, one adjoining to **Mr. Ellery's** near the Church 30'x200', the other in Broad St. by **Capt. Lloyd's** 28'x180'. Inquire of **Mrs. Hamerton**, near the Church.

On Easter Monday, at the house of **Mrs. Eldridge** on the Green, there will be cockfighting.

Large parcel of household goods to be sold at a large warehouse behind **Col. Fenwicke's** house on the Bay.

All persons indebted to **Wm. Russel**, Hatter, are desired to pay their debts immediately as he intends to depart the province quickly.

To be sold a cargo of slaves imported in the *Berkley Galby*, **Perregrine Stockdell**, Commander, from Africa.

Runaway from the plantation of **Charles Odinfells**, at the southward, by Port Royal River, an Irish servant man, named **Patrick Devyero**. He's middle sized, fresh colored, with black hair and a red beard. He had on a brown double breasted jacket, and took with him a round barreled gun, about 3 1/2" in the barrel.

To be sold by **Benjamin Schenckingh**, a plantation in Goose Creek Parish containing 800 acres, commonly known by the name Boo-Chaw, 2 miles from Goose Creek Bridge, etc.

3 March 1733

At night, on Thursday last, his Excellency was pleased to entertain the ladies with a ball which opened by **Lord Forester** and **Miss Peggy Johnson**. Also the windows in the town were illuminated, etc. (it being her Majesty's birthday).

To be sold a plantation containing 664 acres on Wadmalaw Island. Inquire of **Henry Peronneau, Jun.** in Charlestown.

Whereas a tract of 400 acres of land was granted to **Roger Goffe** on the 23rd day of July, 1711, and he afterwards sold same to **Daniel Deane**, deceased. Reward offered for deed showing sale between **Goffe** and **Deane** by **Thomas Ellery**.

A very good Negro woman, brought up in washing and working with two Negro boys for sale at the late house of **Thomas Bartram**, deceased.

A corner lot on the north side of Tradd St., near **Mr. Young's**, the Joiner, to be sold. Inquire of **Jacob Motte** on the Bay.

Strayed from **Mr. Wm. Williamson's** plantation, a large bay gelding.

To be sold, a lot on the Green, 52'x104'. Inquire of **Issac Lewis** in Charlestown.

10 March 1733

Abraham du Buc, a French Roman Catholic, and **Edward Gilbert**, two prisoners who were committed to our jail for felony and broke away and took shelter in the vast woods to the southward, where they continued committing disorders and supporting themselves by killing the horses and cattle of the distant planters, besides which we hear the Frenchman by going to St. Augustine and enticing the Spanish Indians to join them, might be further hurtful to the province of Georgia. **Mr. Oglethorp**, who is now encamped near where the new town is to be, being informed that they had killed a horse belonging to **Mr. John Musgrave** and hovered about that neighborhood sent out a search party which overtook them at the Ojekee River, in their way to St. Augustine, having surprized them, they surrendered and were brought to **Mr. Oglethorp** who sent them to Beaufort where on Monday last they were placed in the custody of the Provost Marshall.

All persons indebted to **Capt. Thomas Boone** of Pond Pond deceased, are desired to pay same to **Mrs. Anne Boone**, Administratrix.

To be sold on the 19th, household goods, cattle, etc. belonging to **John Elliot**, deceased, at Stono. Executors **Thomas Elliott**, son of **Thomas Elliott**, **Thomas Elliott** and **Thomas Farr**.

All persons indebted to **Joshua Morgan**, Brewer are desired to pay by the 25th of April as he desires to depart the province in a short time.

Runaway from **Stephen Ford** of John's Island about 10 months ago, an Indian wench named **Sarah**, about 22 years of age, middle stature, well set, is supposed to be gone over to Hobkoy in man's apparel. She is pretty well qualified for a house wench, and has a cow lick on the hair of her forehead. Whoever brings her to **Stephen Ford** or **Thomas Fleming** in Charlestown shall receive a reward.

Notice given to all persons not to hire Negroes belonging to **Nicholas Trott** viz. **Cussie** and **Beavour**, two Chaulkers and **Anselm** a bricklayer without agreeing with **Nicholas Trott** or **Sarah**, his wife.

All persons indebted to **Mathew Brown** of Charlestown are desired to pay as he intends to depart this province very speedily.

To be let, two large tenements in Broad St. Inquire of **J o h n Breton**.

Lost on the 5th, in or near Dorchester, bound up in a letter, the sum of Ł431, together with an account and receipt signed by **Mr. Tidmarsh**. Also contains bill entitled "to the **Major**

40

Wickham." Whoever brings the same to Mr. James Postell in Dorchester or to John Mason, late schoolmaster, there shall receive a reward.

Runaway from Mr. John Bee, Jun. a Negro wench named Kate, formerly belonging to Bastian Hugoe, and lately taken in execution and publicly sold. Bring to John Bee, Sen. in Charlestown for reward.

To be sold a house 33'x20' with land 96' in depth in Tradd St. next door to Dr. Moody's. Inquire of Henry Saltus or James Ballentine, living in the said house.

To be sold, to the highest bidder on 5 April at the dwelling house of John Dart, in Charlestown, part of the town lot #7 belonging to the estate of Robert Tradd, deceased, situated near the Bay and fronting southerly upon Tradd St.; the easternmost parcel of which has a very large store house upon it, now in possession of Mr. Atkin, merchant, the other piece has a two story dwelling house, etc. Inquire of the Executors Miles Brewton and Thomas Lamboll.

17 March 1733
Last week married in St. Thomas Parish, Mr. John Strahan, 70 years of age and Naomi Painter, age sixty.

The several creditors of the late Benjamin Schenckingh, deceased are desired to bring their accounts to Mess. Thomas Clifford and William Dry for discharge of their debt.

On Thursday arrived George Walker from Providence.

Delivered by mistake from on Board, Capt. William Watkinson, a case with a Bureau in it directed Captain Gascoign. Bring to Thomas Gadsden.

Stolen out of the stable of George Nicholas, in Dorchester, a hunting saddle and a bay gelding. Also another bay gelding strayed from his pasture at Woodbury Plantation near Dorchester.

Peter Precour, Master of Arts, is arrived in the province but a small time and willing to acquaint the public that he teaches French and Latin tongues and his spouse mounts and paints fans and will learn to draw, they live on the Green, at the House of Thomas Farless in Dock St.

Wm. Baker desires to depart this province in about 50 days and wants to settle accounts.

24 March 1733

On Wednesday, **Gabriel Manigault**, was chosen a Member of the Commons House of Assembly for Charlestown in place of **Robert Hume**, lately gone from the province.

(This issue contains a very long description of an account of a voyage to Georgia submitted by S. E. Trip, was taken by writer with **George Ducat**, and **John Ballantine** with 4 Negroes who in a canoe set off from Lloyd's Bridge for Georgia. The letter contains a very detailed account of life and conditions of the early Georgia settlement.)

Eloped from her husband, the wife of **Charles Forrester**, husband advises that he will not be responsible for her debts.

To be sold 1100 acres on Combee River, on the easternmost side of Warnell's Creek. Inquire of **John Page** at Tooboodoo.

Lent by **Joseph Massey**, the first volume of Harrison's Lexicon Technicum. The person to whom it was lent is desired to return it.

To be sold 175 acres, being a part of a tract of 1055 acres, lying on the Beach in the Parish of Christ Church, joining the lands of **James Paine** and **Benjamin Laws**. Inquire of **Rowland Vaughns** in Charlestown.

To be sold on the 8th of April by **Issac Nicholls**, at public vendue, a piece of land joining to the **Widow Scriven's** House in Charlestown. Containing 35' front by 190' depth. Inquire of **Henry Bedon**.

All persons having any demands on the Estate of **Jonathan Main**, deceased are desired to give their accounts to Richard Wigg.

Creditors of **Charles Burnham**, deceased, are desired as soon as possible to send their demands on his estate to **Mrs. Anne Elliott**, to be left with **Thomas Fleming** in Charlestown.

Whereas **Sarah Webb**, on the 5th of Sept. last, did put herself apprentice to **Tho. Henning** to serve him in this Province for 4 years and whereas some evil minded person has enticed her from her duty and given her a sum of money under the pretense that she could pay the same and become free, namely £42 3s 9d contrary to the Act. Reward offered from **Anne**, the wife and attorney of **Thomas Henning** for evidence concerning who gave **Sarah Webb** the money and harbored her.

31 March 1733

Died on Friday, the 23rd, **John Herbert** sole commissioner of the Indian Trade, a his Plantation on Goose Creek, very much lamented for his good qualities, etc.

John Mackenzie and **John Laurens** chosen Church Wardens for the year ensuing.

On Wednesday last, **Thomas Dale**, M.D. was married to **Mrs. Mary Brewton** at St. Philip's Church in Charlestown.

Notice by **Sarah Hirst** that she will not administer the estate of her husband **John Hirst**, deceased.

Thomas Lloyd has for sale on the Bay, the best English white Severn salt.

Stolen or strayed from the pasture of **Charles Hill**, up the Path, a gray mare, Bring to **Richard Hill** for reward.

Meeting to be held at **Thomas Batefellow's** at the New Market House in Charlestown for the purpose of establishing a Society on St. George's Day.

7 April 1733

All persons having any demands on the estate of **Mr. Mungo Welsh**, deceased are desired to present them to the administrator of his estate; **James Crokatt**.

14 April 1733

A Negro and an Indian house-wench to be sold or hired by the year. Inquire of **Wm. Cleiland** in Charlestown.

To be sold by **David Crawford**, at **Mr. Daniel Crawford's** store on Broad Street, tobacco, snuff, pig-tail, etc.

Runaway on the 12th in a small canoe, from the plantation of **William Cattell**, two white servant men, one is a carpenter, about 23 years of age, has short black hair, middle sized and is a Welsh countryman, named **William Merick** and had on a tar'd snuff colored coat, with a checkered shirt. The other's name is **Mullarrey Gill**, about 18 years of age with short dark hair, he had on a checkered shirt, with a brown coat and one broken leg. Bring to **William Cattell, Jun.** in Charlestown or to the plantation of the Master.

Runaway from Charlestown, 3 Negro Sawyers belonging to **Mrs. Catherine Bettisom**, named **Primus, Venture** and **Syphax**. Bring to **Mr. Chardon** or **Mrs. Bettison** for reward **Mrs. Bettison** has for sale good cypress shingles.

Runaway from **Andrew Allen's** plantation at Goose Creek a Mustee fellow about 18 named **J o e**. For reward bring to said plantation or to **Andrew Allen's** in Charlestown.

To be sold house with 2200 acres within 2 miles of Georgetown. Inquire of **Thomas Bolling** in Georgetown.

All persons indebted to **Mrs. Mary Saurean** are desired to pay their debts or to be sued.

To be let a dwelling house, garden, orchard with a great quantity of fruit, etc. near **Dr. Gibson's**. Inquire of **Joseph Moody**.

Stolen or strayed from **Daniel Welsbuysen**, two horses. One was brought up in the Indian Country and sold by one Barker.

To be sold on Board the Snow *Judith*, **Capt. Jeremiah Pearce**, a cargo of Negro slaves imported from the Gold Coast and Angola by **Richard Hill** and Company.

Runaway from **Capt. Thomas Bailey**, a servant man named **Robert Broke**, age about 25 years, and speaks broad Scotts. Bring to **James Smallwood** in Charlestown for reward.

21 April 1733
The house that **Robert Austin** now lives in is to be let, inquire of **John Breton**, he going next week to live in the Stone House on the Bay by whom is sold all sorts of iron ware.

All persons indebted to the estate of **Joseph Lee**, late of Charlestown, deceased, are desired to pay same to **Mrs. Isabel Lee**, sole executrix. Also a new two story house with six fire rooms to be let by the **Widow Lee**.

Runaway from **John Moore**, an old Negro woman named **Juba**, formerly belonging to **Mr. Richard Roe**, deceased. Reward paid by **John Moore**.

The Speech of **Hon. Francis Yonge** to His Excellency the Governor and His Majesty's Honorable Council, April 19, 1733 and ordered printed in the Gazette discusses deeds done by **Dr. Cooper, Mr. Greme**, and **Mr. Vaughan** for which they are presently confined and evidently causing some feuds in the Province. Speaker says that **Dr. Cooper's** commitment is for superintending the Deputy Surveyor in laying out lands contrary to law and the Governor's warrants which tends to create litigious disputes. **Mr. Greme's** commitment is for that he, an attorney at law, did sign a writ against **John Brown Messenger** of the House, directed to the Provost Marshall, at the suit of **Thomas Cooper**, etc. That of **Mr. Rowland Vaughan**, is for an open and notorious affront and contempt offered the House, by serving a Writ of Habeas Corpus on **John Brown**, messenger, when he was actually in the execution of his Office, on the business of the House, with his rod in his hand.

28 April 1733
In the Upper House of Assembly, April 20, 1733 Present His Excellency the Governor, The Honorables **William Bull, Alexander Skene, Francis Yonge, James Kinlock, John Fenwicke, Thomas Waring, Robert Wright**, and **John Hamerton** considered petition of **Thomas Cooper, James Greme**, and **Rowland Vaughan** now in custody, for relief. They were discharged from custody.

St. George's Society created, **John Bayley** chosen President. They had an elegant supper at house of **Robert Roper**.

On Wednesday night, **Mrs. Godin** was delivered of a dead child by **Dr. Dale** and is now in a fair way to recovery.

Runaway from **John Richards**, on the 19th, a white servant man named **John Mathews**, 18 years of age, short, thick and well set, with very short hair, a black complexion and Pock - fretten. Was wearing a pair of ozenbrig trousers and shirt, a pea jacket lined with blue, an old pair of pumps and a fox skin cap. Bring to his master or **James Fowler** in Charlestown.

To be sold a corner lot in Charlestown, over against **Mr. Brandt's** 100' front on Broad Street and 200' on the street that runs from Ashley River to the Broad Path. Apply to Thomas Heyward on James Island.

Mr. William Laflerre desires to leave the province soon and wants all accounts of James LeChantree, deceased settled as he is impowered to handle the affairs of this estate.

Tract of land to be sold containing 900 acres, joining on the horse shoe Savannah in Pon Pon. Inquire of Joseph Mackey.

To be sold - 1800 acres with a good dwelling house 30' in length and 26' in breadth, etc.   Situated on the mouth of Winyaw River about 7 miles from Georgetown.   Inquire of Daniel and Thomas Laroche who are impowered to dispose of the same.

5 May 1733
Cargo of slaves just imported in the Brigt. *Betty's Hope*, Edward Little, Commander from Africa for sale by Jenys and Baker.

Runaway 3 weeks ago, a Negro man named Hampshire, belonging to Mrs. Elizabeth Bampfield.

Good Dorchester ale, in bottles, just imported to be sold by John Champneys of Charlest

Just imported from London, by Captain Baker, to be sold by Thomas Gates in Thomas Elliott's Alley a choice parcel of red herrings.

Whereas I have been informed by people through several parts of the country that there has been a malicious report that I have left off trade this is to advise that I sell desks, chests, clock cases, cabinet ware etc. William Carwithen.

This is to inform Thomas Stubbs, born at Liverpool in Lancashire, if he be in this province, to come immediately to Charlestown, to Thomas Averred on board the *John and Phoebe* Snow to hear something to his advantage.

All persons who have demands on the estate of Joseph Chambers, deceased are desired to bring their accounts to James Rawlings, administrator.

On Sunday last, arrived (in Capt. Allen's from London) in good health, Joseph Wragg one of his Majesty's Hon. Council of this Province, with his Lady.

Common House of Assembly accuses Robert Wright, Chief Justice of the Province with violations of their privileges because of his actions in granting two writs upon an action of debt one at the suit of James Greme, the other by Rowland Vaughan against John Brown, the Messenger of the House, etc.

12 May 1733
Glass ware, stone-line-marble ware and earthen ware, Bristol beer, etc. sold by William Randal in Elliott's store.

The trustees for establishing the colony of Georgia desiring the raising of silk in the Carolinas and Georgia offer to buy silk balls. Bring to Mr. Amatis in Broad Street, Charlestown.

Whereas Dr. Edward Orde has discontinued his business at Ferry Town on Ashley River he asks that all debts be paid or be sued by Charles Pinckney.

Bohea and green tea sold by Mrs. Hamerton near the Church who also offers for sale a lot of land in Charlestown joining Capt. Lloyd's in Broad Street. 28'x180'.

On Thursday last, James St. John was discharged the custody of the Messenger of the Commons House of Assembly.

19 May 1733
To be sold at the Quarter House, 26 cows and calves and some sheep. All persons indebted to the late Mrs. Rebecca Croft, are desired to pay the same to herself, or Mrs. Patridge at the Quarter House.

All persons indebted to the estate of Wm. Morgan, Brewer, deceased are desired to pay the same to Mrs. Eliz. Morgan, administratrix. All persons are desired not to pay any sums to Joshua Morgan.

To be let, the house belonging to Wm. Pinckney, at the upper end of the Alley, adjoining to his Excellency. Inquire of Mrs. Henning at Mr. Breton's House near the Church.

Runaway from Mrs. Elizabeth Dill on James Island, a young Negro wench named Orinda.

Two tracts of land to be sold, being cypress swamp, lying in Colleton County, joining to Mr. Tho. Elliott's the son of Mr. Tho. Elliott. Inquire of Mr. Hezekiah or William Enms.

26 May 1733

Capt. William Davis, Commander of the Snow *Weldon*, offers for sale at Mr. Wragg's Wharf, a small sortment of tin ware, Dorsetshire Beer in casks, etc.

To be sold on the west side of Steed Creek, a stock of cattle and horses belonging to the Estate of Mr. Peter Cattell, Deceased, etc. Inquire of Wm. Cattell and Catherine Cattell.

Runaway from Alex. Vanderdussen's Plantation at Goose Creek, a Negro man named Thomas Butler, the famous pushing and dancing master.

To be sold a white servant boy, age 16, with 5 years to serve. Agree with Jermyn or Charles Wright.

The Brigt. *Bever*, Benjamin Christian, Master, now lying at Motte's Bridge accepting cargo and passengers.

To be sold 500 acres, 8 miles from Dorchester. Inquire of George Austin.

2 June 1733

Contains lengthy description of Oglethorp's movements and Indian meetings.

Richard Hill sells new quart bottles.

At Dr. Breton's new house, the upper end of Broad Street young ladies are boarded by Mrs. Salter, where they may be taught music.

All indebted to the estate of William Cheatham, merchant deceased must pay Edw. Simpson at Ashley Ferry or John Champneys in Charlestown or be sued by Charles Pinckney.

Creditors of the late Michael Macnamar of Strawberry, deceased, are desired to send in their accounts to Edw.

Simpson at Ashley Ferry or **James LeBas** at Wattboo. **Edw. Simpson**, adm.

Runaway from **Andrew Allen's** Plantation called Old Barns a Negro fellow. Bring to the Plantation or **Andrew Allen** in Charlestown for reward.

To be sold by **James Savineau**, 1000 acres. Inquire of **John Laurens**, Sadler.

9 June 1733

To be sold a young Negro woman and two children. Inquire of **Sophia Hume**.

To be sold by **Thomas Thompson**, Commander of the Combe *Pink*, now lying at **Mr. Pinckney's** wharf, a young white man servant who served his time as a gardener. Age between 14 and 15.

Choice parcel of Gold Coast slaves to be sold by **Thomas Walker** in Charlestown at **John Fraser's**. Imported in the sloop *Retriece* from Jamaica.

Runaway on the 14th of last month, a Mustee wench, that may be taken for an Indian, about 20 years of age, etc. Bring to **James Mackewn** at Stono for a reward.

At the sign of the two brewers in Church Street over against **Capt. Brewton's** to be sold strong and table beer. **Joshua Morgan**.

To be sold house and slaves belonging to estate of **Capt. John Gittens**, deceased. For more information inquire of the executors **Capt. Robert Austin**, merchant, on the Bay, **Daniel Crawford**, Merchant in Broad Street, and **Henry Gibbs** in Church Street. By **James Greeme**.

Whereas **Mrs. Elizabeth Morgan** has advertised that no person pay any sums of money to **Joshua Morgan**. He therefore hopes all persons will resort to the said **Eliz.** for his late Father's debts without any demand on him. But asks that persons indebted to him on his own private and separate accounts pay the same to him. **Joshua Morgan**.

16 June 1733

Tuesday last, special court for admiralty met for trying **Ed-**

ward Little, Commander of the Brigt. *Betty's Hope*, for killing Roger Davis, his cabin boy, age about 14 or 15 by giving him 3 or 4 strokes on the head with his cane, on tne coast of Calabar and died 14 or 15 days after.   Three witnesses swore that the boy complained his head hurt because the Captain hit him.   The boy had said that "he neither could, nor would forgive him" and desired that a letter be written to his mother stating the Captain had killed him.   The Doctor said he only had a small bump on his head and that death came because of a fever on board that had killed several.   M r .   L a n e the 2nd Mate was in the cabin at the time of the hitting and swore the Capt. gave him 3 or 4 blows, with a split cane, without a ferrel at the end, and bound with twine, on his shoulders, but did not see him struck on the head and believes fever and not blows caused his death.   The Chief mate gave the same evidence and they gave the Capt. the character of a very human man, a good Captain, and never struck the boy before. Several gentlemen called gave him an extraordinary character. After a trial of 3 hours, he was acquitted.

The same day a Negro about 14 or 15 belonging to Mr. Batchelor in this town dropped down and died immediately.

For sale negroes imported in the Ship *Cate*, William Kennedy, Commander.

To be let a large stone dwelling house at Willtown. Inquire of John Dart in Charlestown.

To be let dwelling house with 2 summer houses, commonly called the Summer-Houses. Inquire of Joseph Shute in Charlestown.

A house to be let on the Bay where M r s . H o g g lived, next door to John Bee. Inquire of Miles Brewton.

Joseph Sleigh, Master of the Ship *Totness* sailing for London.

To be sold by John Raven, Hen. Perroneau, Jun. and James Osmond, (executor to Col. Andrew Hall, deceased) an island to the southward commonly called Seabrook's Island where Mr. Joseph Seabrook now resides containing 1354 acres.

Runaway from Dr. Samuel Steven's plantation at Wesloe Savannah above Dorchester a Negro man named Pompey of Callanber, etc.

23 June 1733

Any who have demands on the estate of **Col. John Herbert,** deceased are desired to present them to **Thomas Clifford,** adm. And whereas there are many who have many small debts owed to the deceased for surveying throughout the country, they are desired to pay them.

Just imported in the *Pearl*, **Capt. Thompson** from London with assortment of European and India goods. To be sold by **Daniel Crawford** at his store on Broad Street.

The Sloop *Swift* sails for Cape Fear in 8 days, **Brabazon Pierce,** Commander.

To be sold 2 tracts of land, one joining land of **Mr. Tho. Farr** and **Col. John Palmer** at Stono. Treat with **Mrs. Elizabeth Francis** or **Joseph Wilkinson.**

Taken up an old Negro man named Jack, speaks very good English. Inquire of **Thomas Holman** near Ashley Ferry.

30 June 1733

Mr. Oglethorpe arrived here and was received with the greatest demonstrations of joy. **Mr. Samuel Grey,** one of the new comers, has had license to quit the colony, and to go into Carolina, where he is said to have a plantation.

On Monday last, died the Lady of the **Hon. Col. Broughton.** A lady of great piety and charity.

7 July 1733

While **Oglethorp** was in Charlestown an Indian near our town shot himself. His uncle who is the war king of the Forks and his friends finding him dead blamed the English. **King Tomo Chi Chi** being informed of the uproar and persuaded that it could not be the English attempted to quiet them. The Uncle continued in a great rage but **Tomo Chi Chi** bared his breast, and said to him if you will kill any body, kill me, for I am an Englishman. This pacified them and an investigation showed the boy had been in despair for several days and asked several Indians to shoot him and an Indian boy saw him put the muzzle to his chin and pull the trigger with his great toe.

Runaway from his master, **Thomas Fairchild,** in Charlestown, a Negro fellow.

Rum from Barbados and Gold Coast slaves sold by **Ribton Hutchinson.**

European goods sold by public vendue at Ashley Ferry by **Edward Simpson. By Stephen Proctor.**

14 July 1733
Thursday last one **Elliott** was committed to our jail for breaking open a chest at Santee, and stealing 200 L.

Last week, one **William Hanser**, was committed to jail for stealing 53 L from **Capt. Hatton** an Indian trader. The said **Hanser** is supposed to have counterfeited letters of credit from Europe.

The same day one **John Jones**, belonging to **Capt. Paul** bound for London, as he was rowing from a ship in the harbor, missed his stroke, tumbled over board and drowned. It is supposed he was in liquor.

Runaway from **Uriah Edwards** of Dorchester a new Negro girl named **Juno** about 14 or 15. etc. Lately imported to **Joseph Wragg.**

Runaway from **William Harvey** of Charlestown a Mustee Negro woman named **Diana** age aboui 21, formerly belonging to **Mrs. Mary Pike** at Goose Creek.

To be sold 150 acres of land on Black River, within a mile of the Church and 12 miles from Georgetown. Apply to **John Lane** on Black River.

At the school of **Adam Battin**, deceased in Church Street, are still taught by another who has taken the school, English, French, Latin, arithmetic and writing by **Thomas Ker.**

Choice cargo of Gambia slaves for sale imported in the ship *Scipio*, **William Gordon**, Commander by **Jenys and Baker.**

21 July 1733
To be sold at **Capt. Robert Austin's** on the Bay, choice claret imported in the *Betty* from Glasgow, Scotch coal, and good Madeira wine by **Alexander Nisbett.**

Stolen or strayed from **Capt. Donning's** batture, a dapple gray horse. Bring to **William Holmes** at Peach Hill or **Capt. Wil-**

liam Sanders at Cyprus shall be rewarded by me. **Brent Farrel.**

To be sold a plantation containing 1000 acres, formerly belonging to **William Moore**, deceased on Black River, Winneau having 200 head of cattle, 30 horses, etc. Inquire of **Samuel Eveleigh** in Charlestown or **John Wallis** at Winneau.

To be let a large commodious house, etc. situated at the north end of the Bay. Inquire of **Joseph Wragg**, merchant.

A tract of land to be sold on Winneau River, 3 miles below Georgetown, containing 480 acres where formerly lived **Joseph Walters**. Inquire of **John Shepherd** in Charlestown.

All persons indebted to the estate of **Joseph Miller**, late of Charlestown, Taylor, deceased or to **Alexander Smith**, while in company with **M i l l e r** , are desired to pay their debts or be prosecuted. By **James Greme.**

Peter Villepontoux has received a patent from His Excellency, for a machine used to clean rice and has entered into a partnership with **Samuel Holmes** for making these machines for those who are interested in purchasing them.

On July 20 arrived **Capt. Moore** in about 12 weeks from London having lost his main top mast by bad weather.

28 July 1733

To be sold parcel of Negroes by **Joseph Wragg & Co.**, imported in the Ship *Shepherd*, **Simon Ford**, Commander, from Angola.

4 lots containing 1/2 acre each lot at Childsberry Town to be sold by **Moreau Sarrazin.**

All persons having demands on the estate of **Adam Battin**, Schoolmaster, deceased are desired to bring their accounts to **Hugh Evans** of Charlestown, adm.

Whereas the wife of **William Coote** has eloped from her husband on Thursday taking with her money and goods. All persons are warned not to deal with her on her husband's account.

Whereas **Thomas Levingstone**, apprentice to **Henry Bedon** of Charlestown, Joiner, has absented himself from his Master.

Reward offered. Also salt and molasses for sale by Bedon.

Land to be sold containing 500 acres, 2 miles from Pond Pond Ferry and Capt. Matthews Store. Inquire of William or Henry Levingstone.

4 August 1733

On the 25th of July, a barn belonging to Thomas Bullin was struck with lightning and burnt to the ground.

William Swinton was made naval officer of the Port of Georgetown, Winyaw.

On Monday arrived here Capt. Davis. Five days out of St. Augustine, who saw evidence of a Spanish Man-of-War sinking in the Gulf of Florida. The ship was bound from Vera Cruz to Cadiz.

Runaway from Henry Fletcher of Savannah, Georgia in a canoe from the Port Royal barracks, a man servant named James Hewitt, aged about 35 years, a thin man about 5'4", and was formerly a schoolmaster in New England, and understands something of sea affairs, and had on when he went away a very handsome chocolate colored coat and pair of breeches, a black waistcoat. He is either in these clothes or a sailor's habit. Also at the same time, and from the same person ran away Tho. Holemark, about 5'8", aged about 25, is very much marked with the smallpox and is by trade a cloggmaker but has been employed at selling and sawing timber. Had on when he went away, a light colored drab coat, with flat metal buttons, and a blue pair of breeches. He had on these clothes or a sailor's habit. If captured return to James Oglethorp in Georgia or the Provost Marshall in Charlestown for reward. By Charles Pinckney.

To be sold by William Dry a plantation about 2 miles from Goose Creek Bridge, a brick dwelling house, with well-stocked fish pond (pearch, roach, pike, eel, and catfish). orchard of apple and peach trees, damn ponds, etc. etc.

Good quart bottles sold by Nick. Harris, Victualer in Charlestown. Sold by John Lining, Orange, Cinnamon and Aniseed waters, and wine.

All persons indebted to **Daniel Green,Esq.** of Charlestown are desired to pay their debts to **Mrs. Elizabeth Green,** his wife and attorney or be sued by **James Greme.**

All persons having demands on the Estate of **Dr. Peter Murray,** deceased are desired to pay **Gillson Clapp** in Charlestown or **Mrs. Murray** at Dorchester.

Runaway for nearly two years, sawyers, belonging to **Roger Saunders.**

Strayed about 14 months ago from **James Cochran's** plantation at Tooboodoo, a tall bay gelding. Whoever brings him to the plantation at Tooboodoo or to **Abraham Graham's** near Willtown shall be rewarded.

Stolen or strayed from Charlestown Green, a bay mare belonging to **John Joor** in Charlestown.

11 August 1733

For sale plantation containing 150 acres in Wampu by **James Stewart. John Laurens,** sadler, in Charlestown has for sale a very neat chariot.

To be sold a tract of land lying on Berrisford's Creek on Wando River. Inquire of **Henry Bedon** in Charlestown or **Thomas Bagiss** in the Country.

Whereas **John Wainwright,** apprentice to **Thomas Sesion** of Charlestown, Joiner did with **Richard Beach,** apprentice to **Nathaniel Ford,** shipwright at Hobkey, runaway from their masters a reward is offered.

18 August 1733

Horse stolen or strayed from **John Brand's** pasture.

Lost between Goose Creek and Charlestown a green silk knit purse marked with white, **N. Moore** having in it 33 pistoles, 3 double doubloons and 5 moldores. Whoever finds it should bring it to **Nathaniel Moore** or in his absence **William Dry** for a gratuity.

25 August 1733

Last week, one **James Ballenis,** an Indian Trader, coming from Savannah town, dropped from his horse and died suddenly.

Also a Negro man belonging to **Thomas Fleming** of Charlestown, killed the overseer with an axe. He was hanged yesterday.

Notice given to the debtors of the store at Willtown that **John Dart**, **Thomas Binford** and **James Smyth** are co-partners that Smyth has transferred his interest to Dart and Binford and debts are to be paid to them only.

Bound for England, Holland, or elsewhere the *Success* Snow, **Capt. Gerald Fitzgerald**. For freight agree with **Richard Hill**.

1 September 1733

To be sold at William Cattell's Landing on Ashley River, household goods, slaves, etc. belonging to the estate of **Col. Ramsey**, deceased.

Good English dwarf peas and molasses sold by **Wm. Linthwait** on Broad Street.

To be sold by **Capt. Rick Shubrick**, a very large moving beausert to be seen at **Godin** and **Guerard's** store on the Bay.

All persons having any demands on the estate of **John Smith** deceased (commonly called **Gunpowder Smith**) settle with **Nicholas Haines** or **Jeremiah Milner**, administrators.

8 September 1733

Whereas several of the inhabitants of Goose Creek have not reported for their taxes for the repairing of Goose Creek and Hume's bridges, the commissioners will meet again in October at the house of **Edward Keating** where they will receive these returns.

Whereas it has been reported by the Land-Hunting Claim and their Abetters, that there has come to Carolina copies of letters I wrote to the **Rt. Hon. Horatio Walpole** and that I am ashame of them and that is the reason I have not attended the service at the House of Commons for two weeks, I request that these letters be published in the Gazette, etc. By **John Lloyd**.

To be sold at public vendue at **Richard Wright's** Plantation on James Island, all Negroes belonging to the estate of **John Wright**, deceased. All persons indebted to the estate or to pay **Richard Wright**, adm. or be sued.

A place near town called the Rat-Trap and a house in town called the Tanyard to be let. Inquire of **Richard Wright** or **Ribton Hutchinson.**

NEWSPAPER ABSTRACTS - 1734

2 February 1734

Stolen or strayed out of **Paul Mazyck's** Plantation in Goose Creek, about 3 months ago, two horses.

Runaway from a Pettiawger of Charlestown, (which was out away about 6 miles southward of Cape Poman) the 8th of December a tall, swarthy person about 30 years of age named **Samuel Ward** and born in Virginia. Bring to **William Anderson** in Charlestown for a reward.

9 February 1734

To be sold by **Nathanial Nichols**, 100 acres on John's Island bounding on Frost Creek. Inquire of **Christopher Smith** on the Bay.

Runaway, a Negro man named **Bristol**, by trade a Cooper, reward paid by **Richard Hill**.

Samuel Holmes of Charlestown, bricklayer, advertises.

All persons indebted to **John Fenwicke & Co.** are desired to pay at the house of **Thomas Lloyd** in Charlestown. By **Tho. Lamboll.**

To be sold a Negro woman formerly belonging to **Judith Miller**, inquire of **George Ducat's** in Charlestown.

Cypress timber sold by **Joseph Mackey.**

Sugar and coffee sold by **Ebenezer Phillips** in Charlestown.

To be sold at **Mal. Glaze's** Plantation near Dorchester, 24 Negroes, stock, etc. Inquire of **Mal. Glaze** or **Laurence Sanders.**

Peter Horry, merchant at Mrs. Ramsey's on the Bay.

Robert Pringle, merchant on the Bay.

On the 14th to be raffled for at the house of Mrs. Eldridge at the Bowling Green, a pair of coach horses, etc.

Runaway from Mr. Paine's Plantation on Wando Creek, on Saturday, 3 Negro men named Hector, Peter, and Dublin, all of Angola (descriptions given). They carried away Mr. Jeffrie's canoe from his landing.

Also runaway from Mr. Paine's Periouger in Charlestown the 8th of January a white man servant named Francis Burn, about 22 years of age, 5'8", pale face with yellow hair and a thin light colored beard, his clothes was a blue duffle gown and fox skin cap with the tail to it. He was heard of near Santee and said to be on his way to Winyaw. Reward given for Negroes and white servant by James Paine or Daniel Crawford in Broad Street, Charlestown.

To be sold all utensils belonging to a brew-house lately in the possession of Will. Morgan, deceased. Inquire of Samuel Holmes at the said brewhouse on Thread Street in Charlestown. Rowland Vaughan, attorney.

Gazette printed by L. Timothee in Church Street.

16 February 1734
Gelding stolen. Reward offered by Issac Chardon in Charlestown.

To be sold by Benj. Dennis, a 46 acre Plantation near the Quarter-House. Inquire of Benj. Dennis at his lodgings near Mr. Thornton's or Mr. Woolford's on the Bay.

Peter Mourgue, confectioner at the corner house in Elliot's Street near Church Street.

To be sold an island opposite to Charlestown commonly called Hog-1sland. On the island is a new dwelling house built on a high bluff which commands an entire prospect of the harbor from the bar to the town. A delightful wilderness with shady walls and arbours. A garden where all kinds of fruits and vegetables are produced and planted with orange, apple, peach, nectarine, and plum trees. Inquire of Capt. Gascoigne in Charlestown.

Thomas Goodman, watchmaker, from London, gives notice that he lives at Mr. Fowler's in Elliot Street, Charlestown.

23 February 1734

A gentleman in town received a letter from the mate of the ship *Marget*, Richard Waistler, commander dated Bodyes Island (a little island in North Carolina) 24 November 1733 announcing that they left port bound for London on October 28 and were shipwrecked on the 17th of November on the said island, whereby eleven were drowned, among whom were M r s . Welshd or Welthd and her child, Mrs. Howard's daughter and others, etc.

William Ford, commander of the Brigantine *John* has for sale a cargo of Negroes. To be sold part of a town lot on the Dock-Street opposite to Mr. Boyaurds lot.

To be sold island called Temecow, northward of Mr. Mott's Island containing about 810 acres, etc. Inquire of J o s e p h Wragg, James Crokat, Charles Hill, Issac Chardon.

To be sold 500 acres, nine miles from Dorchester. Inquire of George Austin, merchant in Charlestown.

Runaway, a young lusty Negro named Parris, carry to Hugh Wilson at Habskaw Plantation near Mr. Russ over against Mr. George Logan on Wandow River or to me Fran. Le Brasseur.

Runaway last Tuesday with a servant woman a sailor named Richard Ricks, he of middle size, well set, with a full face and of a ruddy complexion, about 26 years of age, had on a corded Dimitty waistcoat and a light wig. The woman's name is Isabelle Shaw, she is of middle size, well set, round visage and a likely face, she had on a deep green Camblet gown and a black hat, she is born at Glasgow, in Scotland and speaks indifferent good English and is about 19 years of age. Bring to Joseph Popson, Taylor, in Middle Street in Charlestown for reward.

2 March 1734

Mr. Dry intends to depart the province soon with his family has for sale his plantations. One by the Quarter-house containing 827 acres, the other by Goose Creek Bridge containing 975 acres.

English goods sold by **Lewis Lormier** and **William Baker** in their store in Church Street against Elliot's Street.

Lydia Viart intends to leave the province soon and wants to settle accounts and sell 3 Negroes. She can be reached at **Daniel Townsen's** in Elliot's Street.

Captain John Gascoigne of the ship *Alborough* asks that his debts be paid.

Pete Horry gives notice that he intends to depart this province by April.

John Lining, merchant in Broad Street.

Strayed from about Dorchester, a brown bay mare. Bring to **Nathanial Wickhan.**

9 March 1734

John Bryan, Farrier from London at the three horseshoes in Church Street undertakes to make a sound cure for distemper, etc.

The creditors of **James Sutton** of Charlestown, Vintner are desired to meet at **Mr. Shepheard's** in Broad Street next Thursday.

To be let a shop and a cellar in Church Street, next door to **Capt. Cross**, inquire of **Capt. Thomas Hanking.**

Any person who has a perianger for sale that will carry between 25 and 40 barrels of rice inquire of **Adam Beauchamp**, or **Mr. Swann's** upon the Bay in Charlestown or at **Mr. Mellichamp's** near Edisto.

Stephen Bedon advertises for the lost half of a 25 L bill.

All persons having demands on the Estate of **Twiedie Somerville**, deceased are desired to bring their accounts to **Sarah Somerville**, his executrix.

All persons indebted to the Estate of the late Jacob Satur, deceased are desired to pay their debts to **Joseph Wragg**, merchant of Charlestown.

Taken up on a large sand bank by the mouth of the Stono River, a large plank boat about 18' having 2 masts etc. Whoever owns the same may apply to **Wm. Hutchinson** living on Folly Island.

Whereas **Mr. Blondel, George Wyss, Mr. Morpbew** in Broad Street and others keep and entertain Negroes and servants, at their masters great damage and whereas **Wm. Matthews, Frank Clin**, servants and **William Watkins**, apprentice to **Hugh Evans**, Taylor in Charlestown, have absented themselves, several times from their master's service. This is to advise them that if they continue this practice they will be dealt with according to law.

On Thursday night the ship *Purrysburgh*, **Captain Fry**, from Rotterdam arrived here with about 100 passengers, 47 of which were Saltzburghers for Georgia after 8 weeks passage from Dover. The Captain and 2 of their ministers came ashore with their conductor, **Mr. von Reck**, a young gentleman of great virtue and good abilities who received from **Mr. Oglethorpe** at the Governor's House directions about settling in Georgia.

16 March 1734

On Tuesday last, a Negro man named **Quash**, belonging to **Roger Moore**, was apprehended at the plantation of **Charles Hawe**. He had been run away for 6 or 7 years. When surrounded he went upstairs over the kitchen, a white man and one of His Excellency's Negroes followed him and shot him in the back as he jumped to the ground. He, nevertheless, ran for over 400 yards before falling. He was taken by cart to prison and will be tried in a few days.

Deserted from Port Royal on the 10th a soldier belonging to **Capt. Massey's** company, named **Peter Howard**, an Irish man, he is a thick well set fellow, about 35 years of age, of dark complexion, wears a white wig, went away either in his Regimental clothes or a dark brown coat. He is 5'7". He is supposed to have taken with him 2 Negroes belonging to **Ensign Farrington**.

To be sold an island called Datha containing 1170 acres in Port Royal County bounding on St. Helena River. Also 460 acres lying up Pon Pon River. Inquire of **J. Boone.**

To be sold by **John Watson** in his store at **Capt. Thomas Lloyds** on the Bay, English sailcloth, he intends to soon depart the province.

To be sold 250 acres within 3 miles of Dorchester. Inquire of **Jourdan Roche,** merchant in Charlestown.

Lost sometime last week in Charlestown four inch sissors and 2 points. Bring to **Edward Weston,** Mason at **Mr. Scull's** in Charlestown.

To be sold by **Daniel Cartwright,** 50 acres adjoining **Wilham Elliot's** land, about 2 miles beyond the Quarter House. Inquire of **Cartwright** up the Path, or with **Thomas Ellery** in Charlestown.

To be sold 223 acres on the west side of James Island, fronting on Stono River. By **James Stobe.**

Stolen or strayed from **William Fuller's** Plantation on Ashley River a dark bay gelding.

Whereas a chaise, several parcels of linen, household goods, plate, and other things were lately stolen from my Plantation near the Quarter House and supposed to be concealed by some evil persons in and about Charlestown. A reward is offered for their discovery. All persons are cautioned against buying my cattle or other things from **Mary Townsend,** my now wife, as I will not allow receipt to be given by her and am not responsible for her debts. **J. Townsend.**

The Court House, lately **Mr. Gignilliat's,** was opened on Wednesday, the 6th where gentlemen may receive good entertainment and lodging by **Charles Shepheard.**

Strayed from Moreton Town or Bare Bluff; two horses. Reward given by **Thomas Ellery** in Charlestown.

23 March 1734
Thomas Clifford of Goose Creek was sworn in as an assistant judge.

To be sold 3 town lots at Willtown. By James Bullock.

All persons indebted to Thomas Fleming, Shopkeeper in Charlestown are desired to pay the same as he desires to leave the trade and move to the country. By Rowland Vaughan.

Whereas Landgrave Thomas Smith desires in July to leave this province and go to settle his lands at Cape Fear, he desires to sell his present lands namely the plantation where he lives containing over 1000 acres with a large brick house, 10 miles from Charlestow by land and 14 by water. Also 600 acres 10 miles from Charlestown, also 1400 acres at Wasansaw about 30 miles from Charlestown, 10,000 acres near Georgetown, [and many other tracts of land].

Runaway from Issac Lesseme on Damel's Island near Charlestown - 4 negro men.

Whereas it has been vigorously affirmed and insinuated by Joseph Towsend and his adherents that Edward Shrewsberry of Charlestown has been guilty of a most notorious felony. That this is a most scandalous and malicious report and it is incumbent upon me as guardian to Mrs. Burnham's children, I am obliged to contradict these reports and that the grand jury has investigated and rejected an indictment, etc. By Edward Shrewsberry.

30 March 1734
(Contains long article regarding James Oglethorpe and Georgia. Mentioned are Paul Jenys, Mr. Von Reck, Dr. Zwilfier, Mr. Musgrove, Capt. Fry, Mr. Gronan, and numerous Indian villages.)

(Also contains a long petition of grievances presented by the grand jury to the Chief Justice - Contains names of grand jurors. Miles Brewton, Thomas Elliot, David Hext, Richard Hill, Joseph Massey, Archibald Young, Daniel Cartwright, Arthur Forster, James Akin, Henry Hy---, Luke Stoursborough (?). James Paine, Anth. Bourneau, the Foreman.

To be sold a plantation upon George Town Neck, a plantation containing 1300 acres, on a pleasant bluff at Black River, belonging to Arthur Forster. Inquire of Arthur Forster living at the Brick Yard near George Town or with **Meredith Hughs** at Winyam or **Wm. Watson** in Charlestown.

All persons indebted to the Estate of Nathaniel Sumner, late of Dorchester, deceased, are advised to pay their debts to **Thomas Way** or **Roger Sumner**, executors.

To be let a tenement at upper end of Broad Street, one of which where **Mr. St. John** now lives. Inquire of **John Breton**.

Reward offered for return of my Negro **Parris** who came home but left again with a chain and spurs on each of his legs. **Fr. Le Breasseur**.

Joseph Michie, Deputy Receiver.

Whereas **William Gascoin** and **Joseph Townsend** have concealed and harbored **Thomas Bond**, bound servant to **Thomas Monce** (also **Moncks**) all persons are forbidden to deal with **Thomas Bond**.

6 April 1734

On Thursday morning last, the run away Negro **Quash** was tried by **Thomas Dale** and **Joseph Fox**, J.P.'s, and **George Ducat**, **Edward Croft**, and **Issac Holmes** (three freeholders) and found guilty of burglary for which he was sentenced to be hanged which sentence was carried out in the afternoon. When he came to the gallows he kneeled down at the foot of the ladder and prayed very devoutly, he again prayed for a very short time after ascending the ladder. After he was dead his head was severed from his body and fixed upon the gallows.

Runaway on the 26th, a Mulatto fellow commonly called **Mulatto Jemmy** has straight black hair, age about 20, speaks good English. Bring to **Mrs. Gale** or **Capt. Beak** in Charlestown. Reward by **Hannah Gale**.

Strayed from **Daniel Welshuysen's** near Landgrave Smith's -- three horses.

To be let, a house on the north end of the Bay called Raper's. Inquire of **Richard Wright**.

All persons indebted for newspapers, ads and other printing to the late **Thomas Whitmarsh**, deceased are desired to pay **Robert Pringle**, adm.

To be sold at **Robert Miller's** Plantation near Dorchester, 4 Negroes. **Mal Glaze** or **Robert Miller.**

All persons indebted to the estate of **John Wright** are desired to pay **Richard Wright**, adm. or be sued.

To be sold by **William Gray**, a plantation in St. Bartholomew's Parish.

John Stephens having built a house for storing rice at Stephen's Bridge, where he now lives, gives notice to all persons having plantations near the head of the Ashley River.

Stolen on the 17th out of **Richard Wright's** pasture, near the landing, an Ozenbrig bag (containing numerous items of clothing and books) supposedly stolen by a Negro. Contact **Matthew Brown** in Charlestown.

To be sold a plantation called Epsom Wells, situated in St. John's Parish on the western branch of Cooper River, containing 400 acres, a dwelling house, orchard with pears, apples, peaches, English cherries, plums and grapes, a stream, a good coach road leading from Charlestown, etc. Inquire of **J. Vicaridge.**

Strayed from **Wm. Stobo's** Plantation near Stomo Church, a large white mare. Bring to **Henry Yonge** at Willtown or **Mr. Stobo.**

This Newspaper printed by **Lewis Timothy** in Church Street.

13 April 1734
Common House of Assembly ratified a number of bills, e.g.
2. Cleaning the Ashley River to make it navigable from Waring's Bridge to Dorchester Bridge and then to Plantation of **Sam. Wragg.**
15. An Act for establishing a ferry at North Edisto River from the place commonly called Point of Pines, belonging to **Paul Grimball** on Edisto Island to **Mrs. Bryan's** Landing near Leadenwaur Creek on Wadmelauw Island.

On Wednesday last a special jury was summoned to inquire into a forcible entry whereof **Mrs. Sarah Somerville, Capt. Edw. Croft, Childerman Croft, Abraham Croft**, and **Edw. Wigg** were accused by **James Greme**, J.P. upon his own view. Yet the Justice Commissioners appointed to repair the

67

platform In the Fort Bastion are Charles Pinkney, Gabriel Manigault, Robert Breuton, Othniel Beale, and Benjamin D'Harrirtte. They are to report to John Finwick and John Ragg.

The annual meeting of St. George Society meets on the 23rd at the home of Mr. Charle Sheppard in Charles town. Tickets to be obtained at Mr. Smallwood's on the bay. John Bassette, secretary.

To be sold on the bay next to Mr. Raypor's house, a town lot running the street where Mr. Charles Pinkney lives. Contact Mr. Rouse, Mr. Charles Codner, or Mr. John Daniel.

Tract of land containing 500 acres for sale about a mile and a half from Captain Matthew Stewart, Ponpon. Contact Henry Livingston in Charles town.

Catalog of medicines lately imported by Daniel Crawford (contains long list of medicine).

All persons indebted to the estate of William Elliott, son of Thomas Elliott deceased are desired to bring in their accounts to Jeremiah Miles of Stono.

20 April 1734
Runaway on the 16th from Captain George McKenzie, a servant man named E o w e n. A welsh man about 24 years of age, speaks bad english, he is a tall fellow, has red hair but cut off. He went away in sailor's clothes and has taken with him a gray suit of clothes. Reward of 14 pounds.

To be sold by I s s a c M a z y c k , J r . in Charles town, a pettiauger.

All persons having goods, parcels or letters for Georgia may apply to Mr. Haynes in Charlestown for free passage.

27 April 1734
St. George Society met and chose officers. Charles Pinkney, president; Thomas Dale and Thomas Monck, stewards; Mr. James Smallwood, treasurer; Mr. John Bassette, secretary.

4 May 1734
All persons indebted to the estate of Captain John King,

deceased, are desired to pay their debts to his executrix, Mrs. **King** in Charles town.

All persons having any demands on the estate of Mr. **Thomas Stitsmith** are desired to bring in their accounts to Mrs. **Anne Stitsmith**, widow and administratrix of his estate.

To be sold 100 head of cattle and young horses and a Rhode Island pacing stallion. 40 head of mares. Treat with **Edward North** at Ponpon or **William Roper** in Charlestown.

To be sold on John's Island - a stock of about 60 head of cattle. Inquire of **Samuel Jones** in Charles town.

To be let - a plantation two miles up the path containing 143 acres and a house, formerly rented by **Mr. David Hext.**

Also to be sold - a plantation on Wando River, 12 miles above town containing 230 acre: a good house with four rooms on a floor. Inquire of **Steven Miller**, shopkeeper in Charles town or **Robert Johnston** or **Charles King** in St. Thomas' Parish. **Robert Johnston** is also of St. Thomas' parish.

To be sold - a negro man, leather dresser by trade by **M r s . Collins** over against the French Church.

The Commissioners for exchanging the old paper currency will attend at **Othnieo Beals**.

11 May 1734
Runaway from his master **Thomas Fairchild** in Charlestown a Negro named **Bristol**.

Whereas **John Bishop** late of Jamaica, sailed from that island in April 1733 with **Capt. Peter Carney** for Havanna and Providence where he left **C a r n e y** and came to this Province, but died soon after his arrival. Any information concerning him contact **Daniel Crawford**.

To be sold a plantation within 4 miles of Charlestown containing 400 acres with landings on the Ashley River and Wapoo Creek. Inquire of **William Cattell, Benjamin Godfrey,** or **Benj. Whitaker.**

To be let a house opposite the meeting house, belonging to **Capt. Geo. Smith**. Inquire of **John Baker** who lives there.

The **Widow Varnod** gives notice that she has set up a French school for young ladies and teaches them all types of embroidery. She lives in the house of **Mr. Doursaint** in Church Street near the French Church.

18 May 1734

Just imported in the *Happy Gilbert*, **Captain William Paul** from London and to be sold by **Robert Pringle** a large quantity of European goods.

Richard Hall, gentleman being lately arrived in this province with 462 bushels of hemp seed and 50 bushels of flack seed for sale.

Runaway on the 30th from his master **John Purkis**, a servant man named **William Clews**, by occupation a file cutter of a short stature, well set, swarthy complexion, pretty much pock marked, short curled hair of brown color and speaks very broad english. Had on a dark gray jacket an ozenbrig shirt and britches, brown stockings, very much broken, and a pair of old shoes.

Sailing for Philadelphia soon, the schooner *Dolphin*, Captain **Hugh Crawford**. Any person interested in sailing shall agree with **Joseph Slute**.

Six slaves for sale. Inquire of **Peter Biret** in Broad Street.

Runaway from **Culcheth Golightly** on John's Island, a young mulatto house wench named **Franke** formerly owned by **Mr. French**. She is known by most people in Charlestown.

25 May 1734

Upon the arrival of **Captain Paul** from London that the news and celebration of marriage between the Prince of Orange and the Princess Royal. **Mr. St. John**, the surveyor general, **Mr. Whitaker, Captain Green**, and about 30 other loyal gentlemen met at the house of **Mr. Jacob Wolford** on the bay on the 20th of May at about 6:00 p.m. where the health of the King, Queen and royal family were drank under the discharge of several guns from on board. **Captain Payne**.

Taken up at **Colonel Waties'** plantation at Santee a negro man about 30 years old.

Runaway from his master **William Lewis**, a Mustee negro man who perhaps will maliciously say he belongs to **Elias Horry** or to **Madam Mayrant**.

Runaway from his master **Samuel Crrigh** at Winyaw, a young negro fellow. Whoever find him shall bring him to his master or to **Mr. Johnson** at Winyaw.

Whereas **Mrs. Justina Moore**, daughter of **Landgrave Smith** has arrived from her settlements at Cape Fear and desires to sell 1000 acres of land fronting Winyaw River bein' the upper part of a barony that **Landgrave Smith** bought of **Governor Daniel**, deceased. She desires to return in a month after this date.

James Mishy, Deputy Secretary, gives notice to several persons hereafter named a pai or grants of land signed by his Excellency, the Governor for them respectively.

Henry Yonge	Captain Ladson
David Allen	Samuel Jones
Malachy Glaze	Robert Taylor
--en Baly	John Scale
John Summers	John Allston - 2 grants
William Cattell- 4 grants	William Williamson
Wiliiam Allston - 2 grants	Joseph Scaly - 2 grants
Johnathan Singletay	James Payne
Stephen Ford - 3 grants	Emanuel Smith - 2 grants
Renee Ravenell	Paul Mazyck - 2 grants
William Greenland	Francis Ladsen
Edward Bellinger - 2 grants	Thomas Huft
Issac Porcher	William Miles
Peter Porcher	A. B. Peroreau
Captain Gadston - 2 grants	James Thompson
Joseph Labruce	John Bee, Jr.
Miles Sweeney	Thomas Ford
Thomas Miles	John McGillivrey
George Farly	Joseph Oulcott
John Lane	George Pawsy
William Westberry	Anthony Pauley
William Swinton	John Splatt
Thomas Caan	Thomas Everson
Captain Ouodeintelis	John Caan
John Cattell	Colonel Paris
Thomas Handlen	Anthony Bonneau, Jr.
John Vicarage - 2 grants	Jeremiah Miles
William McClure	Elizabeth Dedcott

Noah Serre - 3 grants
John Moore
Thomas Butler
Silas Wells
Joseph Boone
Capt. Lloyd
Richard Stevens
William Coat
William Singleton
Peter Robert
Richard Bedon, Jr. - 2
Richard Smith
John Pierce
Silvanos Rich
James Walker
Jacob Jenerette
Jane Bullock
John Hamlen
John Bee, Sr.
Paul Brimbat
John Green
Thomas Brown
Nicholas Mattyson
James Ferguson

Issac Nichols
Benjamin Savage
William Screven 2 grants
George Farley
John Newton - 2
James Baer
Thomas Gadston
Francis Perry
Andrew Renmbert
John Coachmen
Charles Hiil
William Shackleford
Justin Beggon
James Anderson
William Sanders
Alexander Bestoy
John Lopton
Thomas Elliott
Joseph Dingo
William Holman
Anne Elliott
William Bradford
William Spencer

1 June 1734

Mr. Drye moves to his lower plantation by the quarter house so that above Goose Creek Bridge will be sold to the highest bidder on Monday the 29th day of July.

8 June 1734

List of justices of the peace for Berkley County.
Thomas Broughton, President
Joseph Wragg
Thomas Warring
John Hammer, All of His Majesty's Council
Arthur Middleton
Ralph Izord
William Brewell
Alexander Skeene
Francis Yonge
James Kenlock
Robert Wright, Chief Justice
Paul Jenys, Speaker of the Commons, House of Assembly
John Finwick
Thomas Clifford

72

Robert Young, Assistant Justices
James Abercrombie, Attorney General
Tileophious Gregory, Master and Chancery

Thomas Dale
Malachy Glaze
Edmund Bellinger
John Skeene, Register
Charles Pinckney
Gabriel Manigolt
Hoffneil Beale
Robert Brewton
Benjamin L'harriette
Andrew Rutledge
Elias Foislin, Jr.
John Daniel
Peter Padgett
Thomas Ashby
Nathaniel Broughton
Thomas Cordes
William Drive
Peter Taylor
James Moore
John Ouidfield, Jr.
Walter Jeard
Robert Wright, Jr.
John Williams
Richard Finley
Nathaniel Wickom
George Nichols
Richard Warring
William Saunders
Gillison Clapp
William Middleton
Benjamin Warring
Alexander Vanderdusin
John Ouldfield, Sr.
Daniel Welshuisen
Lamgrave Thomas Smith
John Gibbs
John Colleton
John Pariston
Peter Day St. Julien
Daniel Huger
Anthony Bonneau
Charles Russell
Francis Lejeau

Thomas Lamboll
William Elliott, Jr.
Richard Wright
Joseph Blake
Roger Saunders
Andrew Browden
Walter Izord
Edward Thomas
John Walter, Sr.
Charles Hall
Issac Mazyck
James Weterburn
Alexander Paris
Benjamin de la Consee
Benjamin Goddin
Jesse Badenhop
William Saxby
Samuel Eveleigh
Samuel Prioleau
Thomas Gadston
George Smith
Issac Mazyck, Jr.
Tobias Fitch
James Hatell
John Baker
Henry Gibbs
Ripton Hutchinson
Joseph Boone
John Walter, Jr.
William Walter
William Cattell
Thomas Draydon
Richard Fuller
William Fuller, Jr.
Issac Porcher
Samuel Wigfall
Michael Derby
Jacob Bond
Thomas Smith
Thomas Boone
Thomas Barksdale
George Logan
Jonah Collins

Thomas Ferguson
Thomas Monk
Benjamin Savage

Joseph Fox
James Le Bas
Signed J. Witterburn

15 June 1734

All persons indebted to the estate of **Joseph Chambers**, deceased, are desired to pay their debts to **James Rowlings**, Administrator, at the house of **M r . T o b i a s   B a r n e s** in Dorchester.

Runaway from his master **John Vaughn**, bricklayer in Charles town, a negro wench named **Hanna**. She has been seen at **Captain Gadston's** and at **Madame Guyle's** plantations.

To be sold by **Mrs. Sarah Summerville** at her house on the bay a number of negro men boys and girls, a chariot and other items.

Stolen or strayed in November from **Sam Jones**, near Wampoo a black horse and a bay horse. Contact **Samuel Jones** or **David Allen** in Charles town.

Stolen or strayed out of **Mr. James Dalton's** pasture near Dorchester, a bright gray horse belonging lately to **Mr. John Fidlings**. Contact **Mr. Dalton** in Charles town near **Mr. Poinsette's** by **William Carwithen**.

Billiard table to be sold by **William Sirret** at Ashley Ferry. Treat with him or with **William Stroby**.

Whereas **Jonathan Wilkins**, bound apprentice to **Richard Roickles** took leave of his master to go and see his relations at James Island for 1 week and has not yet returned. Reward is offered.

22 June 1734

Taken up on the 16th at my plantation on Cumbabee two negro men by **John Mullryne**.

Runaway from **Ripton Hutchinson** on the bay two Irish indented servants, one called **Richard Lee**, a short well-set fellow with black hair about an inch long, a pale face, he speaks Latin, Portugese and English with a brogue and passes for a student. He had on when he went away an old brown scot coat. The other is named **Thomas Field**. He speaks pretty good English, he had on a frock and leather britches. He is of

74

middle size wears his own hair of a dark brown color and has a little stoop. He is by trade a gardener.

A negro boy aged ten named **Jacob** belonging to **Roger Saunders** missing from the plantation commonly called Hyde Park, lately belonging to **Mr. Thomas Elliott, Sr.**, deceased, on Coccaw Swamp. Bring to the master at his plantation on Ashley River.

Leaving for Philadelphia the schooner *Jolly Bachelor*, **James McDowell**, master and having a good accomodation. Inquire of the master at **Captain Symonds** wharf or with **Mr. George Head** or **Mr. Joseph Skute**.

Lately imported from London and to be sold by **William Morgan** at the house of **Mr. William Watson** on Church Street - European Goods.

29 June 1734

A choice parcel of slaves to be sold by **Benjamin Golden** and **John Guererd**. They were imported in the Brigatene *Isabella* by **Peter Porey**, Commander; they're from Angola.

To be sold at Elliott's Wharf on the schooner *Hopewell*, cedar timbers and Philadelphia flour by **John Conner** at his store on the Wharf.

To be sold Wampee's Savannah plantation, 3 miles from Dorchester containing 1000 acres of land with a piece of land at the foot of the Dorchester Bridge. **J. Walter**.

Runaway the 22nd from their master **William Stirling**, 3 scottish indented servants, one named **Gregory Dembster**, a sturdy well-made fellow who speaks broad scot, by trade a cooper. He had on a brown course camblet coat, a ____ jacket and other britches, a woolen cap and his hair cut. Another **Hugh Forbess**, a most well-made man of a ruddy complexion passes for a student. He had on a blue stuffed westcoat. Another, **James Turnbull**, preaged man with a broad flat nose and speaks English with a brogue. He had on a gray sailor jacket. Bring to **Mr. J. Frazier's** house in Charles town for a reward.

6 July 1734

On Monday last, died here after a few days illness, **George Head**, a gentleman who came here with a cargo from

Philadelphia and Providence in the schooner *Jolly Bachelor*. He was decently buried the same day on the Friends burylng ground.

Being taken up a young negro of middle size, says he belongs to **Mr. John Petry** near **Willtown**.

13 July 1734

Thomas Cooper of Charles town desiring to go out of the province early in the spring desires that his debts be settled.

This is to give notice that **Peter Francis Hext** has received from the government of St. Augustine the sum of 600 pieces of land because there remains money due on account of some negroes that ran away from this province. (The rest is illegible).

Dr. Thomas Cooper has bought the indentures of the two Irish servant advertised by **Mr. Ripton Hutchinson**. They were **Lee** and **Field**. The said doctor offers the same reward for their apprehension that was previously advertised. **Lee** had been bred a scholar and the other had been brought up a gardener and had concealed himself under the name of **Clumtree**. He is making his way to the Creeks having lately been seen at **Mr. Smith's, Ladling Dennis'** plantation near **Mr. Rollins'** on Edisto River.

To be sold a choice parcel of negroes imported by the ship *Amaretto*. **David Jones**, master directly from Africa.

20 July 1734

On Wednesday last, at the Council Chamber before the Governor's council for trying pirates. Came on trial: a Spanish carpenter, **Joseph Delori**; charged with pirate _____ and feloniously receiving goods and effects of **Don Francisco de Heymes** who was murdered. Witnesses were cross examined by **Richard Halem, Esq.** ho was counsel. Petitioner and not **James Greeme** as I was wrongly informed. The defendant was found not guilty.

Whereas **Thomas Butler**, fencing master has run away these two years and has been entertained by several gentlemen about the ferry who pretended not to know he had a master. This is to notify them to bring said **Butler** to Goose Creek or Charlestown by **Alexander Vanderdussen**.

Runaway from **George Haddrell**, in April last, and supposed to be harbored by a person in or near Charles town, a negro woman named **Brilla**. Bring to **Haddrell** at his plantation.

27 July 1734
On Thursday, the 18th, **Mr. Robert Pringell**, merchant in Charles town was married to **Miss Jane Allen**, a beautiful young lady, daughter of **Mr. Andrew Allen**, an eminent merchant in town.

Church wardens **John Laurens, James Husband**, advertise for inhabitants of the parish of St. Phillips and Charles town to pay their fees for relief of the poor.

Also mislaid a case of surgeon's instruments in silver. Please restore them to **Captain William Paul** for a reward.

For sale – a plantation at Black River containing 600 acres. Treat with **Robert Sinckler** at Georgetown or with **John Sinckler** at the said plantation.

To be Sold by **Samuel Swan** – candles at **Mr. Thomas Gates'** store on the bay or at his house in Elliott's Alley.

To be Sold – Madiera wine by **Thomas Gates**.

Sugar sold by **William Roper** on Broad Street.

Stolen out of the house of **Daniel Welshuysen** – a large silver spoon.

Taken Sunday from the Quarter House – a large white pacing horse belonging to **Mr. Ferguson** of Ponpon. Bring to **Dr. Cooper** in Charles town or **Mr. Parker** at Goose Creek for a reward. By **Thomas Cooper**.

3 August 1734
From Georgia – **Thomas Causton** ordered a scale boat, two other boats with twenty-five men to go in search of four Spaniards and seven Indians encountered by our Indians while hunting on St. Simon's Island.

Just imported in the *Friend* Ship, **Captain Compton** from London and sold by **James Crokatt** all kinds of linen.

To be Sold - a choice cargo of negroes imported in the ship *Postboy*, **John McNutt** Commander from Angola, by **Jenys** and **Baker**.

All persons indebted to the estate of **John Ramsey**, late deceased, are desired to pay their debts. Also, the house where **Ramsey** lived on Broad Street in Charles town is due to be sold.

To be Let is a large piece of ground and stable and chaise house. Lying opposite to **Benjamin de l'Conseillere**. Contact **William Scott**, **Thomas Flemming**, and **Thomas Lamboll**.

Plantation containing five hundred acres on the east side of Cooper River, seven miles from Redbank on Murrell's Creek - for sale - treat with **Daniel Jaudon** on said plantation.

All persons indebted to **Edmund Bellinger** are desired to pay their debts.

Just imported to be sold by **Eleazer Phillips** at the corner shop on Elliott's Wharf - sugar.

A Georgia messenger continues to carry parcels and so on to Charles town and thence back to Georgia. Whoever needs to do this may leave the same at **Mr. Haynes'** in Charles town or **Elisha Dobree** in Georgia.

From Savannah, Georgia - **Mssrs. Yomans** and **Ascott** and **Beall** and **Cooper** and other merchants in Charles town bring action before **Thomas Causton**, bailiff and **Thomas Christie**, recorder, alleging that **Elias Dobree**, late of Charles town, merchant has removed from Charles town without paying his debts.

From the parish of St. James in Goose Creek - There notice by order of the commissioners **Tong Bayly**, clerk, there is already due and still due sums of money for bridges finished and others contracted for, such as in **Mr. Morrison's** swamps, **Captain Taylor's** and **Mr. Heumes'**.

10 August 1734
To be let - a very good dwelling house near St. Thomas Parish's church. Inquire of **Mr. Grimstone**, constable in Union Street, Charlestown.

Strayed or stolen from the pasture of **William** Saxby, a bright bay mare belonging to **Mr. John Bennell** on Winyaw, the horse may be known by **Mr. Peter Oliver**, of **Mr. William Elvis Burchers** of Charles town, or bring to the plantation of **Anthony White** on Black River for a reward by **Anthony White**.

Taken out of the house of **Thomas Bolton** on the bay, a silver snuff box in the shape of a shell. Supposed to be stolen by a negro.

Bartholomew Penrose has items for sale at his store in Elliott's Wharf.

Richard Eagles has for sale a plantation joining Dorchester Town, also a plantation at Beach Hill, containing 526 acres adjoining **Mr. John Bee**, Savannah.

17 August 1734
On Tuesday the 15th, died near Ashley River in the 104th year of her age, **Mrs. Elizabeth Baker**. Her maiden name was **Elizabeth Wilson**. She was born in Wilshire in a town called Shruton the 18th of August 1630. She lived in England 27 years, in Barbados 23 years, and in Carolina 54 years. She had 12 children, two of them still being alive, 25 grandchildren and 43 great-grandchildren. The same day she died, one of her great-grandaughters, the spouse of **Colonel Palmer**, was delivered of a child.

On the 14th died the **Reverend Mr. John Witherspoon**, a presbyterian minister at James Island.

Whereas my apprentice **Thomas Holmes** ran away from me Saturday, the 2nd of August any person that apprehends him shall bring him to his master, **William Yomans**, merchant in Charles town, for a reward. The said **Holmes** has transacted debts as my apprentice and without my assent and I have empowered one **George Sharmond** and **Robert Shaw** to receive sums of money so contracted. I am speaking also for my partner, **Mr. Gabriel Escot**.

Mssrs. Carvallo and **Gutteres** have good old Barbados rum for sale.

Note Executed June 23, 1732 - received of **Hugh Evans** the sum of twenty-three pounds ten shillings, the full account between said **Hugh Evans** and **John Blades** and the said **John**

Blades empowers **Hugh Evans** and likewise Mr. **Morgan** to deliver up to **Hugh Evans** the note of hand made to **John Blades** by **Hugh Evans**. Witnesses, Nicholas Llyle and James Lawrlow.

This is to give notice that **William Powell**, of Charles town has moved to the house where Mr. **Richard Franklin** formerly lived at Beaufort, Fort Royal, where gentlemen may at all times find lodging.

Runaway from James St. John, on Tuesday the 18th, an Irish indentured servant named **Thomas Ryan**. A middle sized man about 30 years of age formerly an indentured servant to one **Colonel Smith** in Virginia so says **Ryan**. Had on with him when he went away a brown grogram waistcoat.

24 August 1734

On Friday the 16th died suddenly in the night. **Roger Lownds** who a week before was appointed Lieutenant of His Majesty's Snow *Happy*.

Sunday died, **Doctor Cooper**, a man of good character, and very much regretted.

Yesterday died Mrs. **Baker**, spouse of **John Baker**, an eminent merchant of this town.

The Sloop *Lydia* came into harbor Wednesday bound for Georgia from Philadelphia. They anchored on the evening of the 19th and the next morning in weighing the anchor one of the handpikes broke and gave the mate of the sloop, **Benjamin Newble**, a blow on the right side of his head that caused him to fall and soon expire.

Brought to jail, a Negro boy named **Dublin**, belonging to **Doctor Lewin**.

Lost about 10 days ago out of the house of **Capt. Lloyd**, a silver-hilted sword and a green damask belt with a silver buckle. **Tho. Lloyd**.

Thomas Goodman, Watchmaker from London lives in Elliott's Alley at **Mr. Fowler's**.

A horse stolen or strayed from Mr. **Pen Davis'** pasture.

The Brigantine *Three Sisters*, **Philip Marett**, Master, will sail in 3 weeks. For freight agree with **Thomas Duncan** at **Mr. John Sheppard's** or at his store at **Doctor Kilpatricks**.

To be sold the house where **Mr. Henry Gignilliot** now lives. Treat with **Gabriel Marion** and **Issac Mazyk, Junior**.

John Blades, going back home to England gives a receipt to **Hugh Evans**. **Nicholas Llyle** and **James Low**, witnesses.

31 August 1734

For sale – 50 acre Plantation on Ashley River within a mile of Dorchester with gardens, orchards and wooden dwelling house. Treat with **Daniel Pepper** at said plantation.

For sale – 575 acres on Wando Swamp belonging to **John Alston** – 400 acres of it in rice next to **Mr. John Daniel** and **Mr. Wiggfall's** Plantation. Treat with **Issac Chardon**, merchant in Charlestown or the said **Alston** at Winyaw.

Daniel Pepper advertises for horse taken out of **Mr. Kinlaw's** pasture at Goose Creek.

James Dalton advertises sale of 370 acres. Treat with him at his plantation near Dorchester.

Mr. Godin advertises for an overseer for his plantation at Goose Creek where he dwells. Inquire there or at his house in Charlestown.

7 September 1734

Notice given that **John Wilson** has left a very good fire engine with **John Laurens**, sadler, of Charlestown to be sold for the use of the town.

All persons indebted to the estate of **Solomon Tozer**, deceased, are desired to settle with **Wm. Yeomans** and **Gabr. Escott**, merchants and administrators to the estate in Charlestown.

Sophia Hume offers a reward for the 5th Volume of the Belle Assemble, which dropped out of the chaise up the path about a fortnight ago.

Runaway from **Doctor David Anderson** of Dorchester, a short squat Indian slave named **Betty**, she is very fat has long black hair, and formerly belonged to **Capt. Hatton.**

14 September 1734

Runaway from his Master **Michael Jeanes** of Charlestown, Glazier, on the 9th, an indented servant named **John Whatnell,** being a middle sized man, fair complexion, tender eyed, pretty well set, full faced, quick spoken, had on when he left a yellow-orange colored coat coarse cloth trimmed with black, Ozenbrig trousers, Dimitty jacket, and white garlix shirt.

Whereas **John Pittey** a slim boy about 15 years of age, very much freckled and speaks hoarse, ran away from his master on the 28th of August, he had on when he left an Ozenbrig jacket and trousers. **Thomas Weaver.**

The following certify certain information about **P e t e r Villepontoux** new rice cleaning machine -- **William Wilkins, William Rivers, Issac Lewis, Alex. Spencer, Stephen Russell,** and **Lewis Lormier.**

To be let a house on the Green, the east side of the Church of Charlestown where **Mrs. Hammerton** now lives.

Merchants advertising: **Lewis Lormier** (who intends to depart this province); **John Dart; Cattell & Austin; Richard Hill, Charles Hill.**

Run away from **Joseph Elliot,** a young negro named **Sampson.**

21 September 1734

William Trewin advertises for an overseer.   Apply at his house in Charlestown.

Charles Pinckney informs that contrary to rumor, **James H a s e l l,** late of Barbados has not left this province but lives 25 miles from Charlestown.

Two Negro lads named **Cato** and **Smyrna** ran away from **David Anderson** and **Phillip Ayton.**

To be sold at the house of **Mr. Sureau** at Ashley Ferry on the 8th of October, the plantation of **Francis Yonge** lying between the lands of **Mr. Drayton** and **Mrs. Monger,** being the front of the tract lately purchased by **Mr. Jordan Roche,** containing

296 acres and 20 head of cattle, etc. by **Robert Yonge, Lydia Yonge** attorneys to **Francis Yonge.**

To be sold on the south side of James Island on the 8th of October, a plantation with furnishings, etc. Treat with **N i c h . Smith** on James Island.

Robert Hall, provost marshal advertises that **Robert Rhodes** was discharged as his deputy.

Received on April 4, 1734 of **John Toomer** £40 15 shillings discharging the debt of **John Bruce's** action against him. **James Neale. Francis Dandridge** of Stono Bridge mentioned.

Two Rhode Island stallions for sale by **Edward Vanvelson.**

28 September 1734
Stolen or strayed out of **Mr. Croft's** pasture near Charlestown on the 8th a Sorrel Gelding belonging to **Rowland Vaughan** who has been informed that the gelding has been lately rid of by one of **Mr. Fairchild's** men to Wassamsawer and has been disfigured by having his tail and mane cut to prevent detection.

Brought to jail in Charlestown, 2 Negro lads named **C a t o** and **Smyrna** belonging to **Messrs. Anderson** and **Ayton** at Dorchester.

To be sold by **Thomas Buttler,** a tract of land on the north side of Ashapoo River, about 40 miles from Charlestown containing 1260 acres.

All persons having demands on estate of **James Lewis,** late of Charlestown, Perwig-maker deceased, bring accounts to **Robert Scott** or **Hugh Evans** in Charlestown.

Robert Shaw answers **Wm. Yeomans** ad regarding **Thomas Holmes, Yeoman's** apprentice.

The Brigantine *John,* **Samuel Parsons,** master will sail in a few days for Cape Fair.

5 October 1734
A bright chestnut horse, branded 1W stolen from **Mr. Wragg's** pasture on the 2nd or 3rd.

Notice given not to employ a Negro man named **Primus** a Bricklayer and Plasterer, formerly belonging to **Mr. Mullins** and now to **Geo. Haddrell** without agreeing first with **Mr. Christopher Smith** on the Bay at Charlestown. Runaway from said **Haddrell** on August 23, a Negro woman named **Bella** and harbored in or about Charlestown by some evil inclined persons.

Any white or Negro having a mind to learn the Coopers trade, to correct spoiled wine, and to distill apply to **Peter Birot** who will teach them under reasonable conditions. There will be a certain number of bottles with Clairet at Strawberry Fair to be raffled at **Mr. Gignilliat's** at 61 per dozen.

Whereas **Richard Dearsley** and **Thomas Cawood**, bricklayers did feloniously steal and destroy their indentures from Master **Samuel Holmes** and absconded from service of their master for 7 months and claim they were never indentured. I the said **Holmes** did send to England by **Capt. Francis Baker** of Charlestown and brought back copies of their indentures.

12 October 1734

On Sunday last died **Mr. John Franklin**, a Gentleman of very good behavior which made him esteemed and loved by everyone, and as he died a batchelor, we hear he is much regretted by a young lady with whom he was going to be married, if Death had not taken him away.

Stolen or strayed from Charlestown two bay horses supposed to be at French Santee Ferry where **Mr. Ralph German** lives. Contact **John Fraser** for reward.

To be let a plantation on Wampu Savannah, contact **William** or **Catherine Cattell** on Ashley River.

Whereas I have been informed that several people have made a practice of fetching mud from my marsh between Cooper River and Town Creek, this is to forbid them from doing so. **John Beresford.**

To be sold cod fish, madiera wine, etc. by **Thomas Gates** in Thomas Elliot's Alley.

Mr. Dry intends to leave the province with his family and will sell 200-300 acres of land a little more than a mile above the Quarter House and fronting the Broad Path.

19 October 1734

Issac Chardon moves his merchandise to **Mr. Coleton's** store house upon the Bay.

To be sold 400 acres in St. Thomas Parish, near the Parsonage, and formerly in the possession of **Mr. Sweetman**, and 500 acres in Craven County Santee lying on Wosso Creek part of town lot #250, near the Quaker's Meeting, about 56 acres on Charlestown Neck bounding on the land of **Thomas Gadsden** and a broad path opposite **Col. Blake's** land, etc. Contact **Mrs. Elizabeth Hill.**

Lost about 12 days ago from Mr. Conseillere's Creek, a large cypress canoe, 22'-25' long. Reward by **Richard Hill.**

Just imported in the *Hellena*, **Capt. Seaman** from Scotland and London to be sold by **John Crokatt** and **George Seaman** at their store in Broad Street at the house of **John Ramsey**, deceased, merchandise, etc.

William Glen, hatter of Broad Street wants fox or racoon skins. House is next to one **Mr. Ramsey** lived in.

26 October 1734

Arrived on Wednesday **Captain Hennesey** from Calais.

Runaway from the Governor, a servant man named **James Tood**, a round faced fellow, 5'5 or 5'6 about 27 years pitted with the small pox, and speaks very broad Scots; had on when he went away a brown coat.

Brought to jail in Charleston a likely young Ibo Negro man taken up near **Capt. Charles Russell's**, 100 miles from town near the Congree, speaks no English except to say his name, **Jack.**

All persons indebted to **John Franklin** of Charleston, merchant, deceased are desired to pay **Thomas Cooper**, his administrator.

Merchants having items for sale: **Henry Bedon, Thomas Henning, Hutchinson & Grimke.**

To be sold, a plantation near Hampstead, 5 miles from Charleston, good dwelling house, large garden, with an avenue of orange trees also orchard of quince, apple, peach and nectarine trees, etc. Treat with Edward Simpson in Charleston who intends to leave the country for the recovery of his health. Purchaser can receive credit from William Cattell and Richard Fuller.

Runaway from Gerrat Vander Heyden at Purrysbury about 5 weeks ago, two Negro men one named Prince and the other Cupid. Bring to Vander Hayden or to Richard Woodward at Fort Royal or to Mrs. Yeer in Charleston.

2 November 1734
Parcel of slaves to be sold by Joseph Wragg bought from Angola by the Ship *Speaker*, Henry Flower, Commander.

To be sold by John Lining, opposite to Mr. Crokatt's on Broad Street: cinammon water, mint water, wine, clove water, aniseed and orange waters.

Benjamin Godin to sell goods just imported by the *Maryanne* Capt. Shubrick from London, commander.

To be sold a tract of 500 acres within 2 miles of Dorchester, a hundred cleared, the land adjoins the plantation where Mr. Malachi Glaze formerly lived and to that formerly of Col. Glover's. Treat with Ralph Izard at his plantation at Goose Creek.

9 November 1734
Overseer wanted for Col. Lucas' plantation. Apply to Capt. Beal in Charleston.

Lots for sale in and near George Town Winyas. Treat with Anthony White.

The following merchants advertise the sale of goods from the *Maryanne*: James Crokatt, Yeomans and Escott, Peter Horry at his store by Mr. Mott's, Capt. Robert Austin, William Lasserre, Daniel Greene.

Goods imported in the *St. Anbres*, Robert Robertson Commander from Philadelphia, to be sold at Capt. Lloyd's store on the Bay by Peter Robertson.

Mr. Henry Holt, lately arrived in the province, informs the public that on Monday he intends to open his dancing room at Mrs. Lory's in Church St. (The house belonging to the late

Mr. Lloyd). Holt learned under Mr. Essex, Jr. the most celebrated master's in England and danced a considerable time at both the play houses.

To be sold a tract of land lately belonging to Thomas Rivers, containing 55 acres in St. Andrews Parish, near Ashley River Ferry, butting east and west on lands of John Rivers, north on William Clay and south on Thomas Elliot. Treat with Rowland Vaughan.

Charles Warkem, joiner, late from Boston makes all sorts of tables, desks, book cases and also coffins of the newest fashion. Inquire at his shop in Trade Street, next door to Joseph Moody.

Run away from Thomas Weaver, carpenter, in Charles Town, a white boy named John Petty, he is slim and speaks very hoarse and is much freckled in his face. Bring to Thomas Weaver or Deborah Macoy for a reward.

John and Alexander Rigg advertise goods for sale at their store in Trade Street.

To be sold at the plantation of Col. John Hebert, deceased, cattle, oxen, horses, surveying instruments by his administrator Thomas Clifford.

16 November 1734

Col. Purrys lately arrived from England at Purrysburg in the Ship *Simmon*, with 260 Switsers Protestants and their minister Mr. Chieselle etc.

Lost out of my pocket on Monday last over the little bridge at the north end of town, £300. Richard Wright.

Runaway on the 12th from Hugh Evans, Taylor in Charles Town, a servant man named John Thompson, a Taylor by trade, about 21 years of age, fresh colored, well set, and nigh 6 feet tall, squint eyed, speaks broad Scots and flutters in his speech. He had on when he went away a light colored drop fly coat, light colored worsted stockings a new pair of shoes, and a light colored natural wig.

Wm. Waterland, the present schoolmaster of Wassamsaw school gives notice to gentlemen planters that he provides good reasonable boarding for their children and writing, arithmetic, grammar and English. He does not plan to move soon.

Run away from his master **Joseph Gibben**, a Negro man named **Tony** born in Barbados.

Two hundred acres to be sold by **Anthony Spencer** near Dorchester. Fifty acres for sale within a mile from Dorchester by **Thomas Way.**

Thomas Guild gives notice that he intends to leave the province by the 1st of January.

Run away about 5 weeks ago from **Hugh Campbell** of James Island, a Negro wench named **F l o r a** and has been in Charlestown since. Also a horse stolen out of **Mr. Vaughan's** stable in Charlestown. Bring either to **M r . V a u g h a n,** bricklayer in Charlestown or to **Hugh Campbell.**

23 November 1734

A count of all the vessels that are cleared outwards of the Port of George Town, Winyaw from 1 Nov. 1733 to 1 Nov. 1734.

Ship *Georgia* – **Henry Dawburr** for London
Ship *Tames* – **Yoakley** for London
Ship *Purysburg* – **Joseph Fry** for London
Snow *Young Susannah* – **Thomas Bayler** for London
Snow *Friendship* – **Thomas Goodridge** for London
Snow *Hope* – **Charles Greig** for London
Sloop *Swallow* – **Edward Barker** for Charlestown
Sloop *Defiance* – **John Wells** for Charlestown
Sloop *Richmond* – **Sergeant Smythies** for Philadelphia
Sloop *Dolphin* – **Peter Cumestock** for Philadelphia
Sloop *Orange* – **Benjamin Austin** for Philadelphia
Sloop *Neptune* – **Edward Lightwood** for Philadelphia
Sloop *Dolphin* – **Peter Cumestock** for Boston
Sloop *Winyaw* – **William Beale** for Boston
Sloop *Lucreiss* – **James Rogers** for Boston
Sloop *Swallow* – **Edward Barker** for Philadelphia
Sloop *Success* – **John Higgs** for Bermuda
Scooner *Dolphin* – **James Lusk** for Philadelphia
Brigs *Dove* – **William Hill** for Philadelphia
Brigs *Brogdon* – **John Jones** for Pool
Brigs *Carolina* – **Thomas Hemming** for Bristol

Most of these vessels carried Pitch and Turpentine, some carried tarr, some rice and one fruit.

Entered Inwards

Ship *Neptune* - **Thomas Lloyd** from Philadelphia
Ship *Samuel* - **Hugh Percy** from Philadelphia
Ship *Dorset* - **William Oliver** from London
Ship *Brittania* - **Benjamin Wickham** from Rhode Island
Ship *Vine* - **William Moverly** from Lisbon
Snow *Francis and Anne* - **John Derby** - London & Cork

Entered Out From Charlestown

Sloop *Elizabeth and Sarah* - **William Hilton** for Providence
Sloop *Neptune* - **Edward Lightfoot** for Jamaica
Sloop *Retreive* - **Francis Fubber** for Jamaica
Ship *St. Andrew* - **Robert Robinson** for Cowes
Snow *Francis and Anne* - **John Derby** for Oporto

Cleared for Departure

Brigt. *Whitfield* - **John Harrison** to Bristol
Brigt. *Brogdon* - **John Jones** to Lisbon
Snow *Hope* - **Charles Greig** to London
Brigt. *Charming Molly* - **Henry Forrest** to Lisbon

Brought to jail in Charleston:
On the 18th of Nov. - **Mingo** belonging to **Mr. Charles Jones**.
On the 19th of Nov. - **Hercules** belonging to **James Cockran**.
On the 21st of Nov. - 2 Negro boys named **Cyrus** and **Cojo** belonging to **Mr. John Daniel**.

Goods imported from Bristol in Ship *Matilda*, **John Sanders**, Master, to be sold by **Benjamin Savage & Co.**

To be sold by retail in the Ship *Lark* lying at **Mr. Pinckney's** wharf, by **John Argent** from Providence, a small quantity of salt.

Goods imported in the Ship *Dorsett*, **Wilheim Oliver** from London to be sold by **Yeomans & Escott**.

The house of **Thomas Fleming** will be let, inquire of Mary Betterson.

Run away 4 Negros, one very elderly, named Harry, from Mr. **Alex. Goodby.** Bring to **John Daniel** or jail in Charlestown for reward. They are believed to be harbored at Goose Creek.

Thomas Barnes of Dorchester demands that all of his accounts be paid.

Goods just imported from London to be sold by **Joseph Edward Flower** at his store at Mr. **Brasseurs** on the Bay.

Meeting of St. Andrew's Club to be held on the 30th at house of Mr. **James Kerr**, vintner in Charlestown. By **James Michie**, secretary.

All indebted to estate of **Edward Burnet**, late of Winyaw, deceased, pay **Daniel Laroche**, administrator.

To be let a very handsome house and kitchen with a large garden room near Mr. **Breton's** house at the upper end of Broad Street. Inquire **Laroche** or **Issac Chardon** in Charlestown.

Stolen or strayed out of Charlestown on the 5th of August, a small gelding (long description) **Francis de Brasleur.**

Stolen out of the house of Mrs. **Ruth Witherspoon** on the 24th of Oct a gold girdle buckle marked R.S., a snuff box with Queen Ann's head on it in horn, a parcel of silver and a hat and wig.

Runaway from **Nicholas Matthilion**, blacksmith of Charlestown, a Negro named **Jeilemy.**

30 November 1734
Nathaniel Johnson – Public Register of deeds, etc.

Jacob Abercromby threatens to prosecute anyone cutting down timber from the 44 acre tract of land opposite to Dorchester and formerly in the possession of Mr. **Hill.**

Five-hundred-acre tract for sale on Wadmetton Island and fronting Wadmetton River. Inquire of **Samuel Underhill** on said island.

Goods just imported in the *Samuel* from London to be sold by **Capt. James Reid** at his store in the house of **Wm. Pinckney** on the Bay.

Whereas **Tho.** Laroche of Georgetown intends to depart the Province in March next, all persons indebted to **Dan.** Laroche and Comp. are to pay their debts by the 1st of February.

In order to prevent great inconveniences and charge to all those who have purchased lots in George Town Winyaw by taking separate renunciations of dower from the wife of **Elisha Screven,** Proprietor of the said town Meeting to be held at house of **Thomas Bolem.**

7 December 1734
Goods imported by **John Watson** to be sold at **Capt. Thomas Lloyd's** on the Bay.

To be sold a very good house-wench with her child 18 months old. Inquire of **Mr. Bodycoat** in Charlestown.

The Ship *George,* **John Howell,** Master plans to leave for London. Inquire of **Howell** at his store on Simmons Wharf.

Hugh Butler of Exeter has given up store keeping and desires that all his accounts be paid or they will be sued upon by **Thomas Ellery.**

Tickets for a concert of vocal and instrumental music to be held at the Council Chamber on the 18th may be obtained at **Mr. Roger's** house on Broad Street.

Deserted from the *Neptune,* **Thomas Lloyd,** Master, now lying at **Mr. Elliot's** wharf, 2 men, viz. **John Berner** a North-Country man of middle stature, well-set and talks broad, usually wearing a white wig and a blue fisherman's Pea with a white flannel under jacket. **Joseph Pattison** (an Irishman and Shoemaker by Trade) of short stature, black eyebrows and swarthy complexion, generally wearing a Pea with the skirts cut off and a striped linen under-jacket.

Whereas **Mr. Joseph Townsend** has lately made certain agreements with **Thomas Rose** and **Edward Shrewsbury,** Guardians of the Estate of the infants of **Charles Burnham,** the elder, deceased, delivered into the estate of the said guardians the two plantations of the late Charles Burnham in this Province and slaves:

Cussy	Sam
Boston	Tom
Bristol	Jeffery
Tony	Caesar
Frank	Lucy
Prince	Hagar
Grittah	Betsy
Jenny	Bess
Lilly	Taruzen
Dorothy	Susannah
Sophy	

and 47 cattle and horses. **Mrs. Ann Elliot** has taken into possession several slaves, namely:

Jack
Primus
Paris
Nanny
Dinah.

To be let the house formerly belonging to **Richard Goodwin** on the Green, with a good garden and to be sold a one horse chaise by **Daniel Greene.**

14 December 1734

Goods imported by **John Johnson** to be sold, next door to **Justice Fox's** on the Green.

To be sold, a chariot and 3 coach horses. Inquire of **I s s a c Mazyck, Sen.**

To be sold at public vendue on the second Friday in January in Charleston by **Adam Beauchamp**, 2 tracts of land containing 228 acres a brick house 40 X 30, with cellars, barn, meat house, corn house and kitchen, pidgeon house, stable, large garden and orchard situated in St. John's Parish, 5 miles from Stono Landing and in the possession of **James Stewart.**

To be let the upper part of the house wherein **Hutchinson** and **Grimke** now keep their store on the Bay, consisting of 4 very good rooms, 2 large garrets with a fireplace in one of them, a good kitchen. Inquire at store or of **Ribton Hutchinson** at his house on Union Street.

William Rogers advertises for stolen or strayed horse and advises that he intends to depart the province in February and asks that his accounts be paid.

21 December 1734

The Ship *Sea Nymph*, **Richard Forster**, Master intends to sail for London in 10 days.

Edward Holden, commander of ship *Grayhound* from Africa.

To be sold by **Samuel Jennings** at the house of **Mr. Moreau Sarrazin** in Broad Street, jewelry and 8 fine and curious marble tables.

To be sold part of Lot #64 situated in Church Street, near the Anabaptist Meeting, containing in front 35 feet and in depth 190', being lately enclosed with a very fine broad fence and further improved with a complete brick and painted stable and chaise-house. Inquire of **Richard Hill**.

28 December 1734

(Contains a lengthy list of medicines and herbs) just imported by **Capt. Pick** and to be sold by **Doctor Jacob Moon** near the new market.

To be sold by **Thomas Duncan**, goods imported in the *Prince Fredrick*, **Joseph Wilson**, Master from New York.

Richard Hill advertises sale of stock at Hillsborough Plantation on Old Town Creek.

Cuttery ware such as razors, swords and knives advertised for sale by **James De Veaux**, instrument maker, located next door to **Mr. Robert Humes** in Broad Street.

Mr. Lewis Janvier, goldsmith newly come from London, makes all sorts of small work in gold and silver. He lives at the house of **Mr. Sarrazin** on Broad Street.

On the 10th of January will be sold at public vendue, at the Court House in Broad Street, a collection of curious pictures set in gold frames by **Adam Beauchamp**.

A collection of valuable books lately belonging to **Rev. John Withers** deceased for public sale the first of January next to the house of **Henry Livingston** in Charlestown where a catalogue of said books may be seen.

Whereas **William Sterland** has taken the house belonging to **Moses Benn** in Union Street he gives notice to all gentlemen of a fine billiard table with news sticks and balls at their service. He advises that he has left public business in St. John's Parish and desires that hi accounts be paid. By **Thomas Ellery.**

NEWSPAPER ABSTRACTS - 1735

4 January 1735
The Snow *Eagle*, **John Roberts**, Commander, lying at Stono's Bridge will sail for Boston in one month.

Goods recently imported from London in the *Prince William*, **Capt. Pick** and to be sold by **Peter Payne** at his store over against **Mr. Watson's** in Church Street, Charlestown.

Mr. Peter Chassereau, newly come from London, surveys land and teaches drawing. To be heard of at **Mr. Shepard's** in Broad Street or at **Mr. Lawrence's**, Sadler.

Runaway from **Peter Birot**, a Negro man named **Cato**, age 23, born this country.

To be sold on February 1, 200 acres at Tuckedoo near Young's Plantation. Inquire of **Edward Meredith**.

11 January 1735
For the benefit of **Mr. Satler**, at the Council Chamber on the 22nd, a concert. Tickets to be had at **Stephen Bedon's** or **Mr. Roper's** in Broad Street.

Samuel Everleigh, merchant, desires to leave this province for a short time and asks that his accounts be paid. By **Charles Pinckney**.

Stephen Bedon of Charlestown asks that all those indebted to him pay by March 1. Also those who are indebted jointly to him and **Samuel Fly**.

Benjamin Savage intends to depart the province in April and desires those who are indebted to him to pay.

Runaway from **Richard Freeman** on December 27, a Negro woman named **D a p h n e**, middle aged, has a great many scars on her back and one on her arm. Has a front tooth missing.

Very good lime juice for sale by **Peter Calvat** in the house of Mr. Shrewsbury, carpenter.

On December 21 left on Elliot's Bridge a cask containing (various items). Contact **John Bydon** in Elliot's Street, Charlestown, or **Will Anderson** at Winyaw.

Whereas **Isabella**, wife of **Joseph Watson** of Edisto Island has eloped from her husband, said **Joseph Watson** is no longer responsible for he debts.

Runaway from **Samuel Todd**, on November 26, an indentured servant name **James Hannah**, a well set, swarthy man, speaks good English, had on a old black coat and breeches, white shirt, olive colored waistcoat, old shoes and stockings, old hat and cap. Whoever finds him bring to **T o d d** at **W m . Osborn's** house or to **Jacob Woolford**, on the Bay at Charlestown for a reward.

Also runaway from **Todd** on the 3rd, **Richard Loan**, an elderly looking man, broad faced, very yellow by his jaundice, high nose, thick lips, speaks thick, had on a yellow coat, dirty white shirt, all old clothes.

Also **James Norwood**, well set, fresh colored, short black hair and beard, an old hat, light colored coat with cape, an old black waistcoat, old shoes, stitched on the tops. Reward offered.

John Laurens, saddler of Charlestown intends to leave the province sometimes in May and asks that those indebted to him pay.

To be sold by **Nathan Potter** at **Mr. William Pinckney's**, several Rhode Island pacing horses, etc.

To be sold by **Daniel Crawford** in Broad Street very good Bohea tea. He also requests that his accounts be paid.

All persons indebted to the estate of **R o b e r t   L o w n d e s**, deceased are desired to pay **George Austin** or **William Pinckney**, administrators.

18 January 1735

Alexander Tally intends to depart the province within a fortnight and desires that his accounts be paid.

A wallet containing 35 ₤ was lost between Elliot's Bridge and Stephen Bedon's.

Arithmetic, geometry, etc. taught by a person presently under confinement to anyone who will pay Robert Hale, Provost Marshall ₤45 for his release. By Thomas Ryan.

Mrs. Jane Eldridge advertises a handsome saddle and bridle to anyone who wins a horse race to be run at the Bowling Green House on the first Tuesday in February.

Whereas C. Lowndes proposes settling at Winyaw and intends to sell his lands in Goose Creek, 22 miles from town. Contains 500 acres joining to J. Kindloch.

To be sold a plantation containing 200 acres of land, situated in the Parish of Christ Church near Hobkow. (Describes property). Also 400 acres of land on Port Royal Island on the great river, about 8 miles from Beaufort. Also 1200 acres on the Okiter Creek. Jacob Bond.

On the 24th will be attempted a TRAGEDY, called the Orphan, or The Unhappy Marriage. Tickets sold at Mr. Shepard's.

To be sold a plantation on Wando Neck, 12 miles from Charlestown, containing 620 acres, with a brick house, 11 bearing orange trees, etc. Treat with John Daniel or George Logan.

25 January 1735

Laurence Withers - Perwigmaker in Broadstreet.

John & Alex Rigg - Merchants

Alex Nesbett booking freight on Ship *Speedwell* from Glasgow bound for Lisbon.

John Phareur, master of the Snow *Lake*.

Josiah Smith advertises land for sale at Winyaw on the Sampit River. To be let the tenement where Smith lives by Issac Holmes, merchant.

James Thomson and Peter Oliver - Charlestown butchers ask that there bills be paid.

To be sold on the 1st Tuesday in February at the plantation (late of John Law, deceased) where Mrs. Elizabeth Parrock now lives, Negroes, cattle, grain, etc.

Robert Brewton of Charlestown advertise for strayed canoe lost near Rebellion Road and a small bay horse, stolen or strayed from land belonging to Pr. Yonge near Ashley Ferry which horse was purchased from Jacob Bourneau.

To be sold Hampstead Plantation, 5 miles from Charlestown, large garden, avenue of orange trees, orchard of quince, apple, peach and nectarine trees. Contact John Cheveliet at the Plantation or Fr. Yanam in Charlestown.

To Be Sold:
500 acres on John's Island by William Spencer.
Plantation on Wando Neck with 620 acres by Geo. Logan.
Plantation on Christ Church Parish near Hobkey by Jacob Bond.

1 February 1735
Run Away from the Printer on Wednesday, a Negro boy aged 16 named Landon who formerly belonged to Mr. Haynes Vinter in Charlestown. By Lewis Timothy.

For sale, 4 Negro men who can wet, set, and lay timbers. Contact Griffith Bullard, hatter, in Charlestown.

The Ship *Susannah* ready to sail for London, Andrew Pringle, Master. Contact him or Robert Pringle at his store on the Bay.

Run away from Capt. James Killpatrick, his servant boy aged 15 named James Russell, he is tall and slender, had on when he went away a light colored coat, wears a cap, having hardly any hair on his head.

Hugh Wire intends to depart the province.

Wm. Linthwaite, brazier of Charlestown desires that his debts be paid or he will bring suit by Charles Pinckney.

John Johnson has imported goods from London for sale at Mrs. Flavels in Broad St.

Daniel Crawford asks that all his debts be paid.

John Watson advertises Madeira wine for sale, recently imported by Capt. Morgan, also other goods imported by Capt. Vittrey from London.

John Stevens offers a reward for a silver spoon taken from his house in Dorchester. Contact Stevens or Joseph Moody in Charlestown.

8 February 1735
Thomas Bolton offers goods for sale next door to Mr. Wragg's.

Thomas Rose advertises for a stolen or strayed horse lost about two months ago from Mr. Townsend's yard upon the Green.

Daniel Welshuyen advertises a plantation for sale on Goose Creek.

All obliged to John Fenwicke are requested to pay. Ad by Thomas Lamboll.

Run away about 5 weeks ago from Malachia Glaze near Dorchester, a Negro woman named Obbah - middle sized, speaks good English, formerly belonged to John Lloyd, deceased, when he lived in Charlestown. If found bring to Doctor Moultrie in Charlestown or me, Malachia Glaze.

15 February 1735
Just imported in the Pearl Galley, Jason Vaughan, a choice parcel of Gold Coast and Angola slaves by Richard Hill.

James Abercomby, attorney general for the province gives notice that all duties are to be paid.

Run away on the 29th of December from Capt. Johnson's Plantation (near the Ponds) 4 Negro men named Esham, Exeter, Justice, and Besam. Reward offered, contact Stephen Dyer.

On the 18th will be presented at the Court-room, the Opera of Flora, or Hob in the Well, with dance and pantomine. Tickets at **Mr. Shepard's**.

Plantation Negroes for sale. Contact **Alex. Parris**.

To be sold, 2 Negro women, good house wenches and one Negro experienced with a boat and as a butcher. Inquire of **Mrs. Delamare** or **Mrs. Banpfield**.

All person in possession of any lands belonging to **Mathew Smallwood**, deceased, are desired to give an account thereof to **Edward Bullard**, carpenter of Charlestown, who is the guardian of **Smallwood's** children, the said **Edw. Bullard** desiring to leave this province in March.

To be sold, a 50 acre plantation in Dorchester on the Ashley River with a very good brick dwelling house and also a wooden one. Contact **Mary Pepper** at the said plantation.

All persons indebted to **Mrs. Drayton** are desired to pay the same. **Ann Drayton**.

Mrs. Phillippele Henning advertises that she has set up a school in Church Street in the house of **Mrs. Lormieur** where young ladies will be taught French & English, needle-work, make dresses and all sorts of head clothes after the nicest fashion.

Samuel Holmes advertises two white servants as good bricklayers and plasterers.

To be sold, a plantation on Ashley River, called Hillsborough, containing about 300 acres, 4 miles from Charlestown. Apply to **Mrs. Elizabeth Hill**.

22 February 1735
Issac Chardon asks that his accounts be paid.

To be sold on the 27th at the Plantation of **Mr. George Smith**, late, deceased, upon Ashley River by **Benjamin Savage** and **Thomas Lambold**, administrators of the said deceased.

Runaway in January, a young tall Negro named **Titus**. Contact **Ann King** for reward, near the Market.

To be sold, part of a lot in Tradd St., next door to **Mr. Motte's**, 33'x96' with a brick house thereon 33'x20'. Contact **Mr. Henry Saltus** at Beach Hill or **Mr. Henry Livingston** in Charlestown.

Daniel Bourget, brewer, advertises.

To be let a town lot with a dwelling house lying towards the upper end of Broad St., has eleven fine orange trees being the same ground where the Georgian nursery of trees was raised by **Mr. Paul Amatis**. Contact **Capt. Thomas Heyward** on James Island or **Mr. John Champney** in Charlestown.

1 March 1735
To be sold 50 acres within a mile of Dorchester. Contact **Thomas Way** near Dorchester.

Run Away from **John Whitfield** of Charlestown, a Negro wench named **Moll**, formerly belonging to **Capt. Massey**, having a ring worm mark on her left arm.

Peter Birot offers for sale good Clairet and for return of run away Negro named **Cato** (who has an ear slit).

John Stevenson, painter and glazer, asks that his debts be paid to him as he intends to depart the province to improve his health.

Samuel Holmes, bricklayer and plasterer, advertises for business.

8 March 1735
Strayed about 10 days ago from my plantation near Dorchester, two large bay horses bought from **Mrs. Cath Cattell**, one named Tuscarora has been my constant riding horse for six years and he paces. By **Tho. Gadsden**.

To be sold in Thomas Elliot's Alley, by **Thomas Gates**, old English earthenware, etc.

All persons indebted to the estate of **John Story**, late of Black River in Craven County, deceased, or to his administrator **Peter Smith**, who has lately departed this province are desired to pay their respective debts to **James Gordon** of Winyaw attorney for **Peter Smith** or to **James Michie**, Dep. Secretary in Charlestown.

To be let the whole or part of a house in Church Street where Mr. Panton now lives, having two very good shops in the front, he also has a good servant maid to dispose of, she has 3 1/2 years to serve and was brought up in the country.

To be sold by Nich. Matthisen, blacksmith in Charlestown, good axes, cow and horse bells, ploughs, etc.

To be sold by Joseph Massey part of a town lot, situated on the north side of Tradd Street between the house of Robert Collis and Benj. Massey's, 30 feet front by 200 feet deep.

Run Away from Is. Mazyk, Sen. on the 3rd of January a Negro woman named Hanna, a good seamstress, had on a Scots plad gown and white headcloth on her head. Seen at the Point among Mad. Trott's Negroes. By Issac Mazyk.

Those gentlemen who subscribe toward making the road from Cambre to Port Royal and Purrysburg are desired by us commissioners of the said roads to pay their subscriptions to James Mathews in Charlestown. By Joseph Bryan and Hugh Bryan.

On Lady-Day next will be opened with proper accomodations for boarders the PUBLICK SCHOOL of Charlestown where will be taught Greek, Latin, Writing, Arithmetic, Merchants Accounts, etc. By Thomas Corbett & William Buchanan.

To be sold by Thomas Ellery a house and garden in Charlestown measuring 50 front by 228' with the house measuring 25'x72' behind Mr. Cooper's adjoining the Meeting Burial Place. Cherry, plums and orange trees to bear this season.

All persons indebted to the estate of Thomas Fairchild, deceased and to John Fairchild and Comp. are desired to pay either John or William Fairchild or be sued by Cl. Pinckney.

Run Away on the 25th of last month from her master, John Vaughan, bricklayer in Charlestown, a Negro wench named Hanna, has been seen at Capt. Gadsden's Plantation where she has a husband.

Stolen or strayed out of Charlestown on the 5th of August last a small bay gelding. Bring to Francis Le Brasseur for reward.

To be sold an island between Cambre and Bull's River, containing 2200 acres. Also for sale 600 acres on Pacosaba Neck within a Tide's work of Beaufort and 500 acres on the Cambre River. Contact **Joseph** or **Hugh Bryan**.

15 March 1735

To be let, a plantation opposite to that of **Charles Hart**. Inquire of **Sophia Hume**.

John Daniels advertises for an overseer who understands sawing.

To be let a tenement on the Green next to the Church in Charlestown, now inhabited by **Thomas Clifford**. Inquire of him or of **Issac Holmes** in Charlestown.

The Governor wants an overseer for his Plantation at Silkhope.

For sale on the 25th at the Plantation of the late **M r . B e n -jamin Godfrey** on Wapoo-Creek, Negro slaves, cattle, horses, plantation tools. His creditors are also asked to present their demands to **Mr. James Smallwood** in Charlestown. By **Benjamin Whitaker**.

To be sold on the head of the Middle Branch of Stono River, about 16 miles from Charlestown, a plantation having 432 acres of land, a great part being in cypress swamp. Treat with **Richard Capers** at the said plantation or with **Thomas Capers** in Charlestown.

22 March 1735

Numerous goods just imported in the *Valez Trader*, **C a p t . Hudson** from London to be sold by **Hutchinson & Grimke** at their store on the Bay next door to **Mr. Woolford's**.

To be sold by **James Crokatt**, half of a lot on the Bay of Charlestown, 126 feet fronting an Alley and 93' fronting the Bay.

Lost or stolen out of the house of **R. Saunders** at Ashley River on the 14th of March, a silver watch on the plate of which was engraved "Hereford" and the inside works "Whitherton Hereford" had to it a three strand silver chain, etc. By **R. Saunders**.

Stolen or strayed from Irish Town at the head of Cooper River, a bright bay gelding. Bring to Irish Town to **John Jollee** or **Peter Secare** at George Town. By **Peter Secare.**

Eleazer Phillips intends to depart the Province this Spring and wants to settle his accounts, such as have forgot to pay for the *South Carolina Weekly Journal* printed by **E l e a z o r Phillips, Jun.**, deceased for six months.

On Tuesday the 25th will be presented at the Court-room the Comedy called The Spanish Fryar or the Double Discovery and on the 27th the same play for the benefit of MONIMIA. Tickets to be had at **Mr. Shepard's** in Broad Street.

Run away from **Mr. Bryan Reily** and **Mr. John Car Michael,** two Irish servants, both talking Scotch, one named **Roger O. Mony,** a tall pock fretten freckle-faced fellow, stooping in the shoulders, his hair cut and wore a linen cap, a dark brown colored coat and waistcoat, battle breeches, and a new pair of Negro shoes. He has a double thumb with two nails on one hand. The other named **Alexander Sinkler,** a short thick well set, burly looking, long brown hair, smooth face, sharp long nose, fresh colored fellow, wearing a dark gray coarse karsey new coat with buttons of the same, a pair of old brown breeches, a pair of gray yarn stockings and a pair of new Negro shoes with 2 or 3 lifts, each of them about 25 years old. They stole from the said masters a new yellow stocked trading gun marked on the plate of the lock "R. Farmer" and sundry other goods. Also runaway two Negro men one named **George** and the other **Derry.** N.B. A hue and cry is gone after them.

29 March 1735

Run Away from on board the Sloop *Neptune,* **E d w a r d Lightwood,** Master, a white servant boy named **John Spring,** about 16 or 17 years, born in Ireland, freckle-faced, well set, had on when he left an Irish Frife coat and dark colored breeches, speaks in brogue.

Lost on March 25, a gold watch belonging to **Wm. Gascoyne,** marked **Robinson Lendon** on the dial plate. The watch was lost somewhere about Mr. Pinckney's bridge, being in company with **Mr. Coite, Mr. Panton, & Mr. Hunter.**

To be let, a tenement in Tho. Elliot's Alley, inquire of **Thomas Gates.**

Found about 3 months ago, about 20 yards of silk, between the Quarter-house and my own. Owner must give color, and sort of silk plus reward for Negroes who found it. **William Elliot, Jun.**

To be sold two tracts of land lying in Chehaw River, one containing 1500 acres, both tracts a tide's work from Port Royal. Also two other tracts – one of 500 acres on Camboke River near **Mr.** Muirain's Plantation, the other 500 acres on the Pon Pon River. Treat with **William Livingston.**

Just imported in the Combe *Pink*, **Capt. Thompson**, commander, and sold by **Alex Logan** at Mrs. **King's** in Broad St., linens, cloths, etc.

To be sold, 3 plantations containing about 700 acres belonging to **Benj.** Godfrey, deceased, fronting on Ashley River & Wapoo Creek. Treat with **James Smallwood** in Charlestown or **Benj. Whitaker.**

Lodgings well furnished and also a large dining room to be let in house wherein **Mssrs.** Jenys & Baker keep their store by **J. Bassnett.**

Bristol bottled cider, Glocester cheese, by **Richard Hill.**

To be sold by **Hugh Butler** several plantations, one called Mount Pleasant, containing 400 acres of good rice land, whereon is 300 acres of cypress trees fit for sawing, also an adjoining 50 acre tract both in Parish of St. John at Wampee and about 3 miles from a landing. Another containing 300 acres lying at English Santee. Another containing 2000 acres of pine land. For particulars inquire of **John Colleton, Don Ravenell, Capt. Robert Taylor,** or **Tho. Ellery.**

Run Away from **Alexander Vander Dussen**, from his plantation at Goose Creek a white man servant named **James** ------. He has robbed his master of 2 diamond rings, one a large table, the other an oval brilliant, both set in silver, also 1 dozen silver spoons and forks marked MVK. He is of short stature, thick set, of a fair complexion, a cut on each side of his cheek, below his mouth. Had on an old light colored drab coat with 5 large silver buttons, under his coat he had on an Osnabrig frock and trousers and shoe boots.

5 April 1735

Run Away on the 1st from Mrs. Mary Stevenson of Charlestown, a servant man named Walter Wallace, a Scotch man, a
painter by trade, he is of a swarthy complexion, low stature
and well set, had on when he left a brown drugget coat and a
blue coat under it.

To be sold a tract of land containing 209 acres with a house,
situated on a bold creek, known by the name of Five Oaks, 2
miles up Quelche's Creek. Treat with Christopher Smith in
Charlestown.

Alexander Parris needs oyster shells and will pay.

Whereas Elizabeth Colleton, the wife of George Colleton, is
eloped from her husband and has sworn his ruin, he gives
notice that he is no longer responsible for her debts.

This is to give notice that on the 7th of December one
Thomas King, and Susanna Brisley, the wife of William
Cashpull of Craven Co. did rob and take from Wm. Cashpull,
a quantity of money, a silver spoon and other goods and sold
said goods. Thomas King is a middle sized man, born in
James Island, a shoemaker by trade, tawny colored, full
faced, a pretty big nose and big legs, had on a white frock
waistcoat and breeches. She is a middle sized woman, has a
mole on each of her cheeks and a mark of a hole made with a
fork in her right cheek, wears a calico gown and linnen pet-
ticoat. By William Cashpull.

To be sold by Mr. George Chicken 1000 acres of land at
Santee, 500 acres of which is on the north side and all in good
swamp.

John Dart announces that he had the honor to be named by a
great number of the inhabitants of Charlestown a candidate for
upcoming election of a member of the Commons in the room
of Gabriel Manigault and asks for votes of members of Assembly for Parish of St. Phillips, Charlestown.

Andrew Duche, potter advertises that he can supply earthenware cheaper than any that can be imported. Visit him at his
place next door but one to Mr. Yeomans or at his Pot-house
on the Bay.

Just imported per Capt. Lee and to be sold by John Watsone at his store on the Bay, a parcel of choice Madiera wine, also red Lisbon wine.

Samuel Eveleigh advertises choice Florence oil, anchovies, etc.

Tho. Lamboll advertises that the interest on the bonds of John Fenwicke and Co. haven't been paid by many parties owing on them.

John Hammerton, Receiver General gives public notice that quitrents in the Province are due to the Crown and the Lord Carteret. He gives notice that he will be at GeorgeTown, Winyaw the 1st of May to receive the rents due in Craven Co., having appointed Thomas Laroche a year ago to receive these rents in that county.

Whereas Mssrs. John Coit and Peter Hunter were advertised in the last paper as being where Wm. Gascoyne was when he lost his gold watch (as he calls it), they ask him to let them know, who was with him he got the watch, and to advertise the number of his watch which remarkedly was not supplied in the ad or else concealed for good purposes. The said Gascoyne has several times pawned the said watch, a reward is offered by Coit & Hunter for information showing the watch was pawned since the advertisement.

12 April 1735
This newspaper printed by Lewis Timothy in Union Street.

John Dart, merchant, elected a member of the House of Commons in place of Gabr. Manigault, public treasurer.

Capt. Rich. Smith, late member of the House for Winyaw, being deceased, an election will be held to fill his place.

To be sold by Hannah Laurans, a piece of ground situated on white Point in Charlestown, between the house where Laurans now lives and land of Peter Leger, cooper; opposite to land of Thomas Lamboll, the back part adjoining to land of Capt. Escott's.

James Murphy intends to depart the province and desires that his accounts be paid.

To be let, the house and garden where James St. John formerly kept his Office, suitable for a small family, inquire of **John Vicaridge** at Mrs. **Daw's** Plantation near Charlestown.

Strayed some time ago out of Pon Pon plantation a bay horse belonging to **John Whitfield**, formerly belonging to **Wm. Colt** of Winyaw.

Joshua Sunders has land for sale at Pon Pon. Treat with him at his house near Mr. Smith's ferry.

Joseph Wragg, merchant of Charlestown has entered into a new copartnership.

Fr. Le Bresseur advertises that a short Negro woman, named **Filledy**, having been sent by him to his plantation in the Country absconded on the 8th.

All persons indebted to the estate of **John Grove**, deceased, are desired to pay their debts to **Elizabeth & Sarah Grove,** administratrixes, and all having any demands on the estate are asked to bring them to **William Grove** at **Joseph Shute's** in Charlestown the said **Eliz.** and **Sarah Grove** intending to leave the province on the 1st of May.

On the 23rd will be the annual meeting of St. George's Society at the house of **Ch. Shepheard** in Broad St. at 10:00 A.M. by **Joseph Bassnett**, Secty.

19 April 1735
Run Away about 2 months ago from **John Whippy** at Edisto Island a new Negro named **F l a n d e r s**, he has been taken up at Mr. James Cochran's Island about a month since.

Elizabeth Wicking advertises that she has a very large bill left in her shop by a woman who attempted to make some small purchases and then ran out when questioned as to how she got the large bill.

Lately imported in the *Baltic Merchant* by **George McKenzie** and to be sold at **John McKenzie's** Store in Broad St., all sorts of goods.

Cleland and Wallace advertise goods for sale at the Widow Kings opposite to the Market in Broad St. Goods imported by Capt. Nicholson.

Edward Massey intends to embark for England if health permits and wants his accounts settled.

John Allen has goods for sale at his store.

Strayed from the Plantation of Thomas Cheesman on the 28th a large bay horse. Bring to Robert Cooper at Goosecreek or Gabriel Escott in Charlestown for reward. To be let a dwelling house on White Point where Coll. Al. Hext now lives. Inquire of Mr. Albert Detmar.

Mssrs. Carvallo and Guteres advertise goods for sale at their store in Broad St.

To be let the house where Rob. Hall now lives. Inquire of Wm. Linthwaite.

Issac Amyand advertises on behalf of the Commons House of Assembly.

26 April 1735

On Tuesday last, came to trial Mr. Bernard, Master of His Majesty's Ship the *Squirrel*, and others, charged with the murder of Captain Gordon. All were acquitted.

Benjamin Whitaker advertises a corner lot for sale in Charlestown, fronting on Church St. 114' and on Dock St. 119' being opposite to the French Church. Inquire of Whitaker at his Plantation on the Albepoo River.

All who have claims on Capt. Richard Smith, late of this province deceased, are asked to bring their accounts to Mrs. Sarah Blakeway, or to Mr. George Logan. Persons indebted to the estate should pay the same to George Logan, Executor.

To be sold a lot on the Bay with a good dwelling house, wherein the Hon. John Hammerton now lives, 50'x210'. Inquire of Sarah Blakeway.

To be sold a tract of land on the west side of Pon Pon River containing 2200 acres within a mile of Parker's Ferry, having a good dwelling house, etc. Inquire of **James Ferguson** on the said plantation or **John Champneys** in Charlestown.

For Philadelphia soon, the Brigatine *Dymond*, **Henry Barter**, Commander, now lying at Mr. Pinckney's Bridge. Persons wanting to ship goods inquire of **Bar. Penrose** or the said Master.

Run Away from **Edward Thomas'** Plantation a Negro man named **Ben** (description) has been waiting man to **John Wright**, deceased, when he was in England. Is supposed to be about town or at or near **Mr. Richard Wright's** Plantation at James Island. He has a sister at Dorchester at **Mr. Tidmarsh's**. Bring him to **Edward Thomas'** Plantation for a reward.

Jacob Bond advertises 200 acres for sale about 4 miles from Charlestown near the Landing where the Men of War carreen.

3 May 1735
Brought to jail at Charlestown - **George**, a run-away Negro boy says he belongs to **Mr. Cloy** of Pon Pon, taken up at Wappow at **Mr. Harvey's** Plantation by one of his Negro men named **Lubb**; also a runaway Negro man taken up at Pon Pon by a Negro man named **Tony**, belonging to **Ryal Spry**.

Mr. Shepard of Broad St. advertises for someone disposed to encourage the exhibition of plays.

Two horses stolen or strayed from Savannah-Town. (description). If found, contact the owner, **George Sommers**, or **Sam Eveleigh** in Charlestown.

On the 29th a cock fight at the house of **Joe Wilks** at Habcaw Ferry. Eleven cocks will fight.

The Negro woman, named **Filledy**, who being concealed by **Th. Lloyd's** Negro man named **Peter River** convicted thereof, etc. **Fr. Le Brasseurt**.

10 May 1735
To be let a town lot with a dwelling house lying towards the upper end of Broad Street with 11 fine orange trees being the same ground whereon the Georgian Nursery of trees were raised by **Paul Armatis**. Inquire of **Thomas Heyward** on James Island or **James Mathews** in Charlestown.

Charles Pinckney has 100 acres for sale near Goose-Creek Bridge and running down between the Church and the Parsonage House to the Creek. Also a corner lot in town containing 80' front on Union St. and 130' on Lock St.

Stolen or strayed from the pasture of Nicholas Trott, near Charlestown, a large white horse, etc. Reward offered by Sarah Trott.

Runaway from the plantation of Thomas Diston, a new middle sized Angola Negro man, he has one fore eye, and was brought lately by Mr. Savage. Reward offered by Joseph Way.

All persons indebted to the estate of John Stevenson, Glazer, late of Charlestown, deceased, are desired to pay their respective debts to Mary Stevenson, widow of John Stevenson.

To be sold a tract of land containing 500 acres in Craven County, Winyaw Parish upon a swamp called Muddy Gully. Inquire of Mrs. Combe or John Combe at Orange Quarters.

To be sold 500 acres situated on Pon Pon upon Horseshoe Savannah. Inquire of Joseph Mackey.

James Smallwood advertises good European goods for sale on the Bay.

To be sold at Mr. Dry's Plantation just above the Quarter-House, a substantial ox wagon, horse wagon, and canoe. Also Negro carpenters for hire by the month.

Saddle stolen from horse left standing before Mr. Ellery's door. If you have any information contact the printer.

A black horse stolen or strayed from the pasture of M r s. Somerville about 2 miles above the Quarter House. Reward by William Pinckney.

All persons indebted to the estate of Doctor Thomas Cooper, deceased are desired to pay to James Killpatrick, executor of his last will. It is also asked that those who borrowed books from the doctor please return them.

Eleazer Phillips intends to depart the province in a little time and has for sale two very good chaises (and many other items).

One thousand, four hundred acre plantation (contains lengthy description), contact **William Lewis** of Winyaw.

Taken up by a Mustee boy belonging to **John McKay**, a small canoe.

One hundred and twenty acres for sale on Wando Neck.   Contact **Thomas Lorry.**

To be let a plantation on James Island formerly belonging to **Mrs. Stow**, al. **Mrs. King.** Contact **Samuel Drake.**

All persons indebted to the estate of **Doctor John Delemore,** deceased, are desired to pay **Katherine Delemore,** administratrix of his estate, as she intends to depart this province.

17 May 1735
To be let a house and garden on Ashley Ferry very convenient for a tavern which has been kept there some time.   Inquire of **Wm. Street** at the said Ferry.

To be sold on the Bay in Charlestown, two tenements, where **Mr. Edw. Croft** now lives. The lot is 33 1/2' front and 50' deep. Contact **Jonathan Drake.**

Gun powder for sale by **Miles Brewton,** Powder Receiver.

Just imported in the London Fregatt, **Capt. John Sutherland,** a choice parcel of Negroes to be sold by **Cleland** and **Wallace.**

B. Roberts advertises portrait painting, engraving, heraldry and house painting.

Notice is given to the following that there are grants of land recorded for them in the Secretary's Office of this Province, (several having lain there for two years, since signing) if the grantees do not apply in 30 days the fees due will be sued upon: **Wm. Miles, John Stewart** 2, **Ja. Summers** 2, **Hen. Toomer** 2, **Th. Boone, Rob. McNut, Wm. Waties** 3, **J. Hearn, J. Stewart, J. Vanderhorst, Eliz. Hendlin, Geo. Dick, Rob. Whitfield, Hugh Campbell, Jos. Way, Th. Blyth, Susanna Williams, Wm. Sanders, Dugald McKickan** 2, **J. Ouldfield, J. Flud, Ezekiel Cox, Coll. J. Purry, Rich. Capers, Ja. Cochran, Tho. Marrit, Wm. Peters, Tho. Dickson, Ed. Edwards, Ed. Meredith, Fr. Harris, Corn. Dupre,**

Eliz. Perryman, ----- Pawley, Th. Elliot, Wm. Holmes, Tho. Hasell, J. Jordan, Wm. Gray, Hen. Wood, Rob. Keith, Aaron Hanscomb, Jos. Hanscourt, J. Witter, Hen. Durant, Wm. Crips, Eliz. Pamor, Rob. How, Geo. Pawley 3, Ben. Perry, J. Seale, J. Handlin, Jo. Bryan, Hanna Burly, Fr. Perry, Tho. Cliford, Ja. Ferguson, J. Lane.

24 May 1735

To be sold on the Bay where Mr. Shrewsbury, carpenter, now lives by Peter Calvett, very good Madeira wine.

For Philadelphia the sloop *Droitwych*, William Glover, Master, ready for freight or passengers, contact Wm. Bradford or go to the sloop at Elliot's Bridge.

Runaway from Miss Ann Tittsmith a Negro man named Harry.

Runaway from Rebecca Flavell, a Negro woman named Pendar, she had the small pox, the white of her eyes are yellow.

Alexander Parris has oyster shells for sale.

Just imported in the *Mary*, Sam Webber, Master from Tophan and to be sold by Bynford & Osmond (assortment of clothes).

Just imported in Capt. Ayres from London and to be sold by John Watsone arrack in quart bottles, and other goods.

Brought to jail in Charlestown, a negro man who says he belongs to Mr. Edward Thomas and a negro man named Phillip brought in by Wm. Bisby of Charlestown who says he belongs to Samuel Stocks of Ashley River.

31 May 1735

Runaway from Wm. Harvey on Saturday the 10th a Mustee Negro wench named, D i a n a , a very good seamstress. She is said to be about Mr. Savage's Plantation.

Edw. Morris desires to leave the province within a month and desires to clear up his accounts. He is also not to be held accountable for deals made by his wife, Anna, and whoever harbors a Negro boy that he bought from Cleland & Wallace, named Shadwell, shall be prosecuted.

Mrs. Grenier living at Mr. Samuel Glazer's in Broad St. does seamstress work.

To be sold in Goose Creek Parish, 10 miles from Charlestown, a Plantation known by the name of Halfway House, a tavern with the same name. Inquire of Wm. Hamilton who lives at the house or James McClelvey living in English Santee.

Hugh Evans, Taylor of Charlestown desires that his debts be paid. Rowland Vaughan.

To be let the house in Middle Street where William Carwithen lately lived near Mr. Poinset's. Inquire of Samuel Fley in Broad St. or Mrs. Carwithen.

Mrs. William Kellaway advertises goods for sale at Mrs. King's on Broad St. Goods just imported from London and Gibraltar by Capt. George Colebatch in the *Charming Phillee* and by Capt. Jacob Ayres from London on the *King George*.

To be let the house where Ebenezer Simmons now lives.

Goods just imported from Bristol on the *Unity*, Charles Smith, Capt., for sale by Benj. Savage.

To be let for 3 years a house and an apartment with a billard table in it adjoining the former in Broad St. Contact Mr. Birot at the sign of the white horse.

To be sold on the north side of the Santee River, about 300 head of cattle. Inquire of Thomas Farr at Stono.

To be sold 1650 acres of land on Ceder Creek on the north side of Santee River. Inquire of Issac Mazyck at Charlestown.

7 June 1735

Brought to jail at Charlestown a Negro fellow, taken up at Mrs. Hill's Plantation by one of her Negroes named Bristol.

Bound for Philadelphia, the Schooner *Dolphin*, James Lusk, Master. For freight or passage agree with Jos. Slute & Comp.

To be sold 800 acres on Goose Creek. Sophia Hume.

All persons indebted to the estate of S o l o m o n   T o z e r, deceased are desired to settle with Messrs. Wm. Yeoman and Gabriel Escott, administrators. By Joseph Moody.

14 June 1735

Whereas certain denominations of the current bills of this province, namely 15 pound, 4 pound, and 3 pounds, have been counterfeited, we the undersigned commissioners order that all bills of these denominations be brought to us by August 7, at the house of **Othniel Beale**, merchant, after which they will no longer be legal tender. **Charles Pinckney, Othniel Beale, Gabriel Monignault, John Champneys, Barry Sanders.**

Sixty cows and calves waiting for the public at Purrysburg. **Peter Taylor, Commissary Gen.**

The following persons may apply at the Secretary's Office for their grants within 30 days – **Peter May, J. Gregory, J. Green, Sarah West, Ifraed Andrew, Tho. Croll, Sam. Small, Hugh Swinton, Geo. Bennison, J. Mackey, Wm. Allen, J. Lane, Thomas Everson, Thomas Sacheverel, Wm. Ladiem, Wm. Waites, J. Allison, Tho. Ferguson, Percival Pawley, Adam Stuart, Charles Jones, J. Duranque, Wm. Cooper, Richard Bland, Henry Ferguson, Robert Fledger.**

Brought to jail in Charlestown, a Negro boy aged about 15 taken up in Charlestown by **Griffith Bullard**, Hatter, said to be brought from Africa in the *Rainbow* Galley, **Richard Morgan**, Captain.

All persons indebted to the estate of **John Stevenson**, Glazier, late of Charlestown, deceased, are desired to settle their accounts. **Charles Pinckney.**

To be sold on July 3rd at the plantation of Mr. Edward Keating, Goose Creek, a stock of cattle, etc.

Richard Tidmarsh of Dorchester complains about "notorious and virulent falsehoods" circulating about him.

Runaway on the 7th from **Experience Hoard**, carpenter in Charlestown a servant named **George Emmerson**, a short well set fellow, black hair, light blue suit of clothes.

Edward Bullard offers goods for sale from the Brigt. *Dymond* from Philadelphia.

To be sold 2 tracts of land lying on Chehaw River, one having 1500 acres the other 800 acres. Also 500 acres on the Cambohe River was Mr. Mulrain's Plantation and 500 acres on the Pon Pon River. By William Livingston.

Taken from a plantation at Goose Creek on the 18th, a dark bay mare. Reward offered by Fran. Le Brasseur.

All persons indebted to the estate of Edward Weekley, Sen., deceased are desired to settle same. Those who have demands on him are desired to bring same to Mr. Baker, Sexton, in Charlestown. Tho. Weekley.

To be sold on Seabrook's Island on Albepoo River a stock of cattle containing about 80 head. Contact John Woodward on Albepoo River, or Richard Woodward at Beauport Town, or in Charlestown with Benj. Whitaker.

To be sold a tract of land containing 400 acres situated on Port Royal Island in the county of Granville butting to the south land belonging to Arthur Dickes and to the west on Port Royal River. Contact Rowland Vaughan at Charlestown.

John Sheppard is removed out of Elliot's Street to Capt. Baker's House in Tradd Street near Mr. Kerr's where he has goods for sale.

Runaway a tall elderly Spanish Negro named Guan, £10 reward offered by Alex. Vander Dussen.

Taken up on the Ashley River in a canoe a Negro fellow named Charles, about 50 or 60 years old, says he belongs to a gentleman named ----- Fuller. The Negro is in jail in Charlestown and the canoe may be had at Mr. Richard Goodwin, smith in Charlestown by paying the charges.

To be sold a piece of land, 2 miles up the path between James Crokatt & Daniel Cartwright's fronting Ashley River and the broad path about 5 yards or more, about 25 or 30 acres cleared. Treat with Richard Cartwright at James Withers on the Bay.

Indian corn to be sold by Giles Holiday on the Bay in Charlestown.

Brought to jail in Charlestown, a Negro named **Issac** taken up at Wappoo per **Priscilla Mongin** of Charlestown.

To be sold a tract of land on the west side of the Pon Pon River containing 2200 acres, within a mile of Parker's Ferry, having a good dwelling house, stores, etc. Contact **James Ferguson** on the Plantation or **John Champneys** in Charlestown.

28 June 1735

Lost about 2 months ago from **Landgrave Smith's** pasture at Goose Creek, a light gray horse. Bring horse to **Landgrave Smith** or to **Edmund Bellingers** at Ashley Ferry or to **Henry Hyrne** at Tooboodon.

Runaway from **Titus Bateman** a young Mustee wench named **Virtue** with a young child of two years suspected to be on the way to Edisto. Bring to me or to **Col. Benj. Waringsan** of Goose Creek or to **Benj. Smith** at **Mr. Crokatt's** in Charlestown.

An apprentice boy named **Israel Andrews** has runaway from his master on the 22nd. He is about 15 years old, had on an Oznabrig jacket and trousers, is of a muddy complexion, short hair of a dark brown color. Reward offered by **Joseph Dopson**, Taylor in Charlestown.

Runaway in March from **Peter Roberts** of Santee, an Eboe Negro man named **Primus**, a little fellow with a very yellow complexion with scars.

Runaway some days past a young Negro fellow named **Tony** (who has a very remarkable great toe on his right foot) and a Mulatto fellow named **Jamey** (belonging to **Mrs. Gale**). Reward offered by **Oth. Beale**.

Slaves from Angola for sale by Joseph Wragg & Co. Imported in the ship *Dove*, **Richard Fothergill**, commander.

Francis Henley and **Barth Dormount**, servants belonging to the right Honorable ----- Trustees in Georgia have taken up in this Province but afterwards received by **John Blakely & Edward Pindergras**. Please bring **Henley** or **Dormount** to me or to **Mr. Chardon** in Charlestown. **Ja. Abercromby**, Counsel for the Trustees.

117

Notice is given that many of the Negroes belong to the Plantations of **John Walters** are continually running away. If found bring them to Dorchester Plantation or to **John Reed**. By Issac Chardon.

5 July 1735

To be sold a very good new copper still very fit for cordial waters at the house of **Doc. Jacob Moon** opposite to **Jeremiah Miller** in Charlestown.

Notice is given that trustees for Georgetown will meet at the house of **Thomas Bolen** in the said town on the 1st Monday of September to give titles for lots. Those inclined to take titles are to contact **Daniel LaRoche** in George-Town.

To be sold by **Thomas Bolton** on the Bay, very good salt, Philadelphia flour, etc.

Brought to jail in Charlestown a Negro fellow named **Scipio** taken up at **Mr. Waring's** Plantation beyond Dorchester.

Plantation overseer sought by **Lt. Governor Nath. Broughton** in St. John's Parish.

Tuesday last **Jas. Abercromley**, his Majesty's Attorney General of this Province set out for Georgia to be at the trial of **Thomas Mellichamp** and **Joshua Turner** suspected of counterfeiting.

12 July 1735

Public notice is given that **Rebecca Maggee**, wife to **Wm. Maggee** is eloped from her husband taking all that belongs to him. He is not responsible for her debts.

Mr. Lewis Janvier, Goldsmith, who lived at **Mr. Sarrazin's** in Broad St. is now moved to the upper end of Elliot's Street where he makes all sorts of fine work in gold and silver.

Brought to jail in Charlestown, a Negro fellow named **Dirk**, belonging to **Charles King**, taken up at **Capt. Brewton's** Plantation by **Frank**, a Portugese fellow.

This is to give notice that the several Negroes belonging to the estate of **William Donning** and **Thomas Donning**, Esqrs. deceased, being 125 in number and all the oxen, sheep, horses, plate, household goods and Plantation tools are to be

118

sold at the Pond's Plantation in Berkley County near Dorchester on the 13th of August. Among the Negroes there are several good carpenters, coopers, smiths, sawyers and shoemakers.

Runaway on June 30th at Mr. William Fuller's Bluff, a Negro girl named **Diana**, about 18, £3 reward offered by **William Fuller.**

Runaway from **Richard Eagles** sometime in May, a Negro wench named **Jeney** and her 3 children, formerly belonging to **Benjamin Godfrey's** estate. Whoever brings to **Mr. Branford's** on Ashley River or to **Richard Eagles** or to jail shall have a £5 reward.

William Kellaway advertises goods for sale at his store on Broad Street.

Whereas the greatest part of Georgetown Winyaw stands upon lands formerly belonging to **John Perry** and now belonging to his daughter **Mary**, the wife of **John Cleland** of Charlestown merchant. Notice is given that these lands are not for sale or for disposal. By order of **Mr. Cleland** and his Lady. **James Greme.**

Two hundred and thirty-three Negroes imported on the Ship *Amoretta*, **David Jones**, master for sale by Benj. Savage & Co.

19 July 1735

To be sold a house with a large garden at the upper end of Broad St., belonging to **Samuel Smith**, butcher, together with a very fine clock. He also asks that all his debts be paid by September 1, as he intends to depart this province. If accounts are not paid suit will be pursued by **James Greme.**

Giles Holliday on the Bay has for sale Mulcovado sugar, molasses, soap, and European goods.

All persons indebted to **Anne Lorry**, deceased, or **William Verplanck** are desired to pay as the said **Verplanck** intends to depart this province.

Runaway from **John Whitfield** a Negro slave called **Kate**, formerly belonging to **Charles Hart**. Whitfield also asks that all debts owing to him be paid at his house in Dorchester or to **Rowland Vaughan** at Charlestown or be sued by **Vaughan**.

To be sold on Wandown Neck, a choice tract of land containing 355 acres fronting the river, 16 miles by water from Charlestown. Deal with **Samuel Bullock** living on the said Wando Neck.

To be sold a tract of land on the north side of Ashley River containing 800 or 900 acres, the front high bluff land, within a mile of Dorchester, being a part of Woodbury Plantation. Inquire of **George Nicholas**, Dorchester, or **Capt. Robert Austin**, merchant in Charlestown.

On the 23rd a quarterly meeting of the St. George's Society, at the house of **William Pinckney**. **John Bassnett**, Secretary.

Gillson Clapp, **Gabriel Escott**, **Rib. Hutchinson**, **Issac Mazyck, Jr.**, and **Edward Croft**, all tax collectors ask that taxes be paid.

26 July 1735

To be sold on the 31st a choice parcel of Negroes imported in the Brig. *Diana*, **Capt. John Malcolme**, directly from the Windward and Gold Coast of Guiana by Benj. Savage & Co.

Molasses by the gallon and white bread by the barrel or pound and a very good chaise horse to be sold by **Samuel Holmes** at his house on Tradd St.

Just imported in the *Mary*, **Capt. Robert Pollixfen** from London and to be sold by **John Johnson** at Mrs. Flavel's in Broad St., a choice parcel of cloths, etc.

The Commissioners of the Parish of St. Phillips, Charlestown, being desirous to meet the commissioners of the Parishes of St. Andrews and St. James Goose Creek, in order to settle the bounds of the broad path of each Parish. **M i l e s Brewton**, **Daniel Greene**, **John Sheppard**.

The Snow *Britannia*, **Tho. Hatton**, Master will sail in 10-14 days. For passage or freight settle with the Master on board his vessel at Stone's Bridge, or with **Messrs. Yeomans** and **Escott**.

2 August 1735

To be sold a plantation containing 200 acres with a very good dwelling house, on Goose Creek, 12 miles by land from Charlestown with 60 head of cattle and some sheep, also a lot in

Charlestown 45x140 lying next to Mrs. Eliz. Fairchild's. Inquire of Daniel Willkuysen at the above mentioned plantation.

To be sold 2 lots in Dorchester Town each containing 45 acres one being known as Lot 11, in the second division of lots, butting east on Joseph Lord's lot, south on Moses Way's lot, west on a division way and north on a range way. The other is number 18 in the 2nd division of lots, being easterly on a division way, southerly on land of Tho. Osgood, Sen., west on the saw-mill land and north on John Steven's land. Inquire of Abraham Satur at his plantation at Santee or Rowland Vaughan in Charlestown.

Bound for Philadelphia, the Billander *Oliver*, Capt. Robert R o b i n s o n, will sail in 10 days. For freight or passage treat with the said Captain on the vessel or Capt. Hugh Percy.

To be sold on Weds. the 6th of August 60 choice slaves imported in the *Faulcon*, Capt. Samuel Sanders directly from Angola in eight weeks by Jenys and Baker.

9 August 1735

On Monday night Capt. Robert Robinson, Master of the Billander, called the *Oliver*, got up and was seen by one of the passengers going to the head of the vessel. In the morning he was reported missing and it is supposed that he fell overboard. A sloop coming up the River last Friday saw sharks tossing up a man in the water, and tearing him to pieces, having on a scotch plaid banyan which was how Robinson was dressed that night.

To be sold a very good Negro, a bricklayer & plasterer by trade, his master leaving on business. Inquire of John Phyps over against the Quakers Meeting, or the Printer.

All persons indebted to Paul de St. Julien before last Christmas are desired to pay the same or be sued.

Whereas Thomas Barker, executor to the estate of Captain Francis Palmer, deceased, desires all persons indebted to the said estate to pay their debts, likewise Dr. Thomas Barker & Co. begs the like favor or they will be sued. By R o w l a n d Vaughan.

This is to give notice that Lawrence Withers, Perukemaker in Broad St. will leave for England the 1st of April and has a large quantity of fine gray hairs by him, which he is willing to work up before he leaves . . . . will furnish Gentlemen good wigs at a much cheaper price . . .

For Philadelphia directly, the Billander *Oliver*, **Capt. Samuel Merchant** will sail next Wednesday. For freight or passage agree with the said captain on board the vessel or with **Capt. Hugh Peiray.**

16 August 1735
Mr. Dry, near the Quarter House, advertises for an overseer and a trusty white man to go in his Pettiaugua.

To be sold a plantation on the head of Wando River, containing 1000 acres, bounding on **Mr. John Russ, John Weskot, Mr. Warnock, Mr. Edwards**, and **John Fogarty's** lands. Inquire of **Richard Hill.**

The executors of the estate of **Dr. Tho. Tittsmith** desire to settle all accounts or suit by **Charles Pinckney.**

Brought in the Snow *Mary*, **Capt. Pollixsen** from London a case marked with a grape, the owner is desired to claim same. Inquire of **John Mittchel**, warsinger at Wragg's wharf.

A list of plats in the Secretary's Office laid aside because of objections. The persons concerned are required to attend at the Council Chamber on the 2nd day of September and remove same. **J. Hammerton,** Sec.

The Honorable Robert Wright	6000
Ja. Hopkins	2 ea. of 150
Wm. Alston	129 + 180
Alex. Smith	700
Wm. Swinton	350
Rich. Perry	1000
Jos. Stanyarn	684 + 400
Dan. Dean	509
Ja. Mathews	690
Andr. Allen	1445
Elias Foissin	700
Ja. Bulloch	866
Wm. Cochran	1200
Benj. Child	602
Dan. Crawford	776

Tho. Clifford	472
Jonath. Bryan	500
Tho. Cooper	650
Arch. Stobo	900
Capt. Wm. Bell	1000
Wm. Yeomans	1100
Dan. Welshuysen	1300
J. Carmichael	525
Ja. Thompson	316 & 299
Col. Palmer	2450
Jos. Seabrook	1212
Ja. Parker	1564
Wm. Mepherson	200 + 400
Joshua Wilks	800
Alex. Parris	2200
Ephm. Payne	500 + 950
Peter Johnson	750
Js. Ferguson	652
J. Peters	180
Cha. Lowndes	2200
Dan. Green	1000
Tho. Butler	566
Jonath. Beltyson	650
Jane Monger	500
Cha. Parker	474
Abr. Graham	612
Sam. Williams	300
Eliz. Pamor	148
Paul Jenings	400
Charlotte Hutchinson	1290
Eliz. Dedcott	204
Amth. White	380
Sol. Middleton	800
Eliz. Raven	500
Edm. Atkins	350
Steph. Bedon	1100
Cath. Laine	250
Wm. Dry	130
Wm. Sanders	314
Dan McGregory	500
Tho. Elliot	575
Wm. Screven	333
J. Musgrove	500–300–300–400
Tho. Witten	527
Is. Grunbal	52
J. Vanderhoeft	400

Job Howes	270
Wm. Hazzard, Jun.	400

To be sold 400 acres in St. Thomas Parish near the parsonage, and formerly in the possession of Mr. Swetman, part of a town lot #250 near the Quakers Meeting, about 56 acres on Charlestown Neck, bounding on the lands of Thomas Godsden and the broad path opposite Col. Blake's land whereon is a new cypress house well finished with a large hall and 4 rooms on a floor, each a chimney, pleasant garden. Inquire of Mrs. Elizabeth Hill.

Richard Hill has choice Barbados and Jamaican rum for sale.

To be sold 210 acres in St. Andrew's Parish joining to Col. Wm. Bull. Inquire of Peter Ginardean or said Plantation.

Brought to jail in Charlestown a Negro named Ocipio taken up by one of Peter Pagett's Negroes at his Plantation, also two Negro fellows named Coffee and Abraham taken up at Mount Pleasant near Mr. J. Gray at the pair of Chuckles by Joseph Prealow.

Grants signed and recorded in the Secretary's Office and ready to be delivered to the following persons: Wm. Alston, Ja. Armstrong, Ja. Atkins, Benj. Avant, Anth. Atkinson 2, Jos. Andrew 2, Pet. Alston, John Abott 2, John Alston, John Atchison, William Allen, Wm. Breckington, Christoph. Bearman, Ja. Baxter, Th. Buston, Is. Bodert, J. Bonin, Tho. Boone, Peter Benoitt, Capt. Geo. Bennison, J. Barnet, Tho. Bosher, Tho. Blythe, Nathaniel Broughton, Richard Bland, Hannah Burnly, Edw. Bullard, Tho. Collier, J. Cook 2, Saml. Commander, Wm. Carwithen, Benthy Coke, Wm. Crawl, Sarah Chamberlain, Tho. Clifford, Wm. Cooper, John Cochran, Ezek. Cox, Is. Chardon, Rich. Capers, James Cochran, Mary Drake, Benj. Dela Counseire, Issac Davids, Abr. Dupont, Ja. Dalton, Ja. Dubose 2, Wm. Donning & Winefred Anderson, Andr. Delavillette, Corn. Dupree, Henry Dwant, Wm. Furguson, Ja. Furguson 2, Tho. Furguson, David Fulton 2, J. Fendin, Elias Fasoin, Tho. Farr, Wm. Fairchild, Jos. Fidler, John Gough, Jos. Garnier, Abr. Graham, Rich. Godfrey, John Gregory, Wm. Greenland, John Green, John Hoddy, Dan. Horry, Fr. Harris, John Harris, Nich. Haynes, Wm. Hendrick, Paul Hamilton 2, Will. Holmes, Is. Holmes, Meredith Hughes, Dan. Jandon, Dan. Jandon, Jun., Henry Jackson, John Knox, Alex. Killpatrick,

Henry Lewis, Is. Lesene 2, John Long, Henry Lewin, Is. Legrand, Geo. Lea, John Leay, Wm. Leander, Andr. Liddell, John Lane, Is. Lewis, Wm. Ladson, Susannah Mayant, Alex. McElroy, Samuel Morris 2, Geo. Mitchel, Abr. Micho, Ja. Martin, Susannah Mayrant, Fra. Murrell, Robt. McNutt, Anth. Mathew, Sen. 2, John McKay, Peter May, Rich. Tho. Morritt, Edw. Meredith, Geo. Oliver, Henry Perroneau 2, Sam. Perroneau, Tho. Powell 2, John Phipp, Percival Pawley, Col. Purry, Ja. Rawlins, George Rivers, John Russ, Benj. Savage, John Splatt, Ja. Sinclear, Nath. Snow 2, Eliz. Screven, John Snow, Wm. Snow, Wm. Swinton 3, Fra. Sureau, Ja. Stewart, Benj. Stiles, Jos. Singletary, Ja. St. John, Capt. Ja. Stewart, Hugh Swinton, Wm. Saunders, Wm. Saxby Sr., John Stewart, Ja. Sutherland, Edw. Thomas, J. Tucker, Wm. Thomas, Elizabeth Varner, George Vincent, Rowland Vaughan, Abr. Warnock, Tho. Westbury, Sarah West, Dan. Welshuysen 2, Eliz. Ward, Susannah William.

Runaway from Goose Creek Point, a Negro man called Trampoes, belonging to Mr. Thomas Wright. Bring to Richard Wright or Mr. Vander Dussen for a reward.

Runaway a few days ago from David Mongin an Angola Negro man named Solo. Bring to David Mongin, watchmaker.

To be sold by Moses Austell at Mrs. Romsey's on the Bay various goods.

23 August 1735
To be sold on November 3, two tracts of land in Goose Creek belonging to C. Lowndes both having 500 acres on adjoining land belonging to James Pindlock. Inquire of Capt. Robert Austin or Thomas Ellery in Charlestown, John Colleton of Fair Lawns or C. Lowndes on the spot.

Dropped by my Negro girl between Mrs. Harris' and Mr. Gooding's house a suit of Flanders laced Head clothes, 2 laced Mobs, 2 laced handkerchiefs. Bring to Elizabeth Lions at Mrs. Harris' for reward.

All persons indebted to the estate of Tho. Fairless, deceased, are desired to pay by Capt. Robert Austin, administrator.

For sale at the Plantation late of Major Tob. Fitch at Goose Creek, a choice parcel of country slaves, most born in this country, also 130 head of cattle, 3 yokes of working oxen, several horses and mares, etc.

For the use of the public is wanted bricks, lime and workmanship to build up the fortifications before the Bay of Charlestown. Please present proposals to **John Fenwicke, Joseph Wragg, Samuel Prioleau, Charles Pinckney, Othniel Beale, Alexander Hext, and Samuel Jones.**

Commissioners **John Fenwicke, William Bull, Joseph Wragg,** and **Miles Brewton** advise public of an Act calling for building the wall along the Bay as required by law by those who claim lots on the Bay, as there is an apprehension of War at this time.

Last Monday, one of the Commissioners having received information from a gentleman in the country that there was a box containing a great number of counterfeit bills in **Capt. Sam. Underwood's** barn on Wadmellan Island, and that **Thomas Millichamp** and one **Morgan** had used the bills in that neighborhood, **William Hamilton,** Constable went Tuesday with an order from the Governor to fetch after and seize the box and a warrant from **Thomas Dale, J.D.** to apprehend the said **Tho. Millichamp,** he went secretly up to **Underwood's** barn and found the said **Millichamp** and **Morgan** cutting and hammering brass, upon their discovery by **Hamilton, Millichamp** immediately fled but was pursued by one of the company and knocked down and taken in the cornfield. **Morgan** likewise attempted to escape but was prevented by the Constable from doing so. The pair had a loaded musket beside them but because they were surprised they were unable to use it. In the barn and house were found counterfeiting materials and in **Millichamp's** pocket book were found counterfeit Ł12 & Ł10 notes. **Mr. Thomas Millichamp** and **Joshua Morgan** were brought to the jail in Charlestown and committed by **Justice Lamboll** for the same crime, on the information of the Magistrates of Georgia.

30 August 1735

Friday morning, the 8th, one **Wm. Nash,** who lives on Pon Pon was at the Quarter House and had in his possession a horse branded G II advertised in several *Gazettes* which said Nash was told that the horse belonged to **Fr. Le Brasseur,** he answered it did not, and rode away on it. Whoever convicts the illegal possessor of this horse shall receive a reward of Ł 20 by **Fr. Le Brasseur.**

To be sold on Sept. 10, 400 choice slaves imported in the *Molly* Galley, Capt. John Carruthers directly from Angola by Benj. Godin.

Runaway from John Reynolds, carpenter near the French-Church in Charlestown a young fellow about 19 named Jonathan Lewellen, he had on when he went away 3 coats, 2 shirts, one pair of Ozenbrigs and one pair of leather breeches, a pair of stockings, 1 pair of pumps and a pair of shoes, one of the coats in white Dowlas, the other a whitish colored cloth and the other a dark colored cotton, £5 reward offered by John Reynolds.

Before me Thomas Dale, J.P. in Berkly Co. personally appeared Dennis Sconell, who being duly sworn says that John Fowler, carpenter and joyner late of Charlestown did give him a promissory note for £75 10s on 7 August 1734 and whereas Sconell did endorse the said note to Sam. Holmes of Charlestown, bricklayer and did receive full satisfaction from Sam. Holmes for said note. Now Sconell says that a few days after signing the said note, one Capt. Finch, one Patrick Hiderwick, one Wm. Gibson, who lives at the sign of the Man in the Companies in Charlestown, which 2 last named came on board the ship commanded by the above F i n c h, then lying in Rebellion Road, the 3 in order to revoke the assignment on the note the said Hiderwick and Gibson told him they came from Richard Hill, merchant on the Bay, etc.

Richard Eagles of Charlestown, merchant demands payment of all debts or suit will follow by Charles Pinckney.

On Saturday last died in Charlestown, Capt. Anthony Math-e w s , an eminent merchant and settler of this Parish, who by his industry, frugality and improvement in mercantile affairs, acquired one of the greatest estates in this country. He first arrived in this province about the year 1680. Now near 55 years hence, and died in his 73rd year, and was decently buried on Monday, last. But what is observable is, that his Pall was supported by six of the ancient inhabitants of this town, hardly one who has been less than 40 years in this Province and whose several ages past together amounted to about 400 years. A sufficient proof that Carolina is not one of the most unhealthy climates on earth.

Whereas a short well set fellow of a ruddy complexion, light sandy hair, who called himself John Eglin, aged about 25-30, being convicted of a felony, made his escape from the Constable in Georgetown, he carried with him a black cloth coat, and a mouse colored Duroy coat, lined with red silk, a short green jacket trimmed with silver or gold, and several Dimery Jackets and enticed with him a short lusty Negro wench, she speaks good English, about 30 years old, supposed to be in men's clothes. £50 reward offered by Dan. and Tho. Laroche at Georgetown, Winyaw or Issac Chardon in Charlestown. He carried with him a light horse, branded on the mounting shoulder with an R backwards joined to an M.

6 September 1735
To be sold the following tracts of land viz. 200 acres on Hilton Head Island bounding to the west on the River Mary and on the north a Creek, 224 acres in Goose Creek Parish bounding to the east on land owned by Mr. Baird to the south of Mr. Pifbreane and on the west by Mr. Brunsons land, 365 acres of land in St. John's Parish about 4 miles from Strawberry bounding on Mr. Harlston and Dr. Martine's lands. Inquire of Roger Moore or Alexander Nisbett.

Brought to jail in Charlestown -- an Ebo Negro girl per Mr. Glaze of Dorchester; Berwick and London, Negro men belonging to Joseph Butler taken up in Charlestown by Wm. Elliot.

Wm. Gibson signs an affidavit denying that he was involved with Patrick Hiderwick in getting a power of attorney from Dennis Sconell and that Sconell's remark, "that the old Son of a Bitch had taken advantage of me by catching me drunk and had tracked me out of the note" that the person to whom Sconell was referring was really unknown etc. [Note: The printer apologies for previously printing the affidavit by Sconell that it was printed through neglect which he was busily employed with other work and he did not notice that it was intended to asperse an eminent merchant of this town, that the mistake was made from ignorance and inadvertency and he begs the persons pardon, he being a man of known modesty and veracity. The truth of the matter comes from the aforegoing affidavit given by Wm. Gibson.] (These affidavits have been condensed appreciably by this compiler.)

To be let the house that John Fairchild lately lived in up the path above the 3 mile post, till February next. Inquire of John or Wm. Fairchild.

Charles Lowndes intending to go to the West Indies as soon as his crop is off desires those he is indebted to, to send their demands to Capt. Green, merchant in Charlestown or to Lowndes Plantation.

R. Saunders and Tho. Bullime advertise that the sale of goods lately belonging to Major Tobias Fitch scheduled at his Plantation in Goose Creek Parish is rescheduled for Sept. 18 because of bad weather.

Runaway a fortnight ago a Negro man Tom, formerly belonging to Mrs. Gale, well known about town, but not for his goodness, 40s reward for his return by Thomas Gadsden.

Bound for any part of Great Britain or Holland the Ship *Hope* Galley she having been very lately new sheathed. Inquire of Master Daniel Reed or Richard Hill for freight or passage.

Bound for Barbados directly, the Sloop, *Sweet Nelly*, Mathew Turpin, Master, for freight or passage agree with the Master or with Gabriel Manigault.

All persons indebted to the estate of John Romsay, deceased, must pay by the 1st of January by order of the executors of his last will and testament - Tho. Flemming, William Scott, Tho. Lamboll.

On Thursday last at Christ-Church Parish died the Reverend Mr. Fullerton, late minister of the said Parish, decently buried Friday.

On Monday evening last Capt. ----- lately master of a Sloop, and a young Toufor of this Town, had a mind to imitate your Gentleman Honor, by a trial of skill at sword and pistol, wherein they rather frightened then hurt each other; and the most melancholy circumstance attending this hardy adventure is that Capt. Quixot has since fainted away several times from a strong imagination of himself being mortally wounded, and having actually killed his antagonist. This grand quarrel, like most others of that sort arose from several pretentions to the favors of a certain fable beauty.

13 September 1735

To be sold by Thomas Hall, a fine Negro woman with her child, she is an excellent cook and washer. Inquire of Hall at his house opposite to the Baptist Meeting in Charlestown.

Brought to jail in Charlestown:

1. **P r i m u s**, a Negro fellow, had on a brown coat, taken up at **Capt. Harris'** Plantation by **John Daniel**.

2. **Primus**, a Negro fellow belonging to **Doff Levity** taken up in Charlestown by **Wm. Partridge**.

3. A Negro boy name unknown, taken up by a Negro fellow belonging to **Col. Parris** named **Cafar**.

To be sold, two tracts of land one on Port Royal Island bounding land of **John Howell** and surveyed for **Alexander Mackey**. The other lying on the south side of Port Royal River and by a Creek called Mackey's Creek, each tract having 500 acres. Inquire of **William Osborn** or **Charles Pinckney**.

Whoever has pretentions to lots in George-Town should give lot number and purchase money to **Dan. Laroche** in said town to have title completed.

Carvalis and **Giutteres** store on Elliot's Street in the house of **Mr. Carwithers**, carpenter, advertises a large assortment of goods including a very good Rhode Island pacing horse.

To be sold on Oct. 23 at the house of **Capt. Richard Smith**, deceased, on Sanpit Creek near Georgetown, Winyaw, 46 choice slaves and household goods. Also it is desired that his accounts be settled contact **George Logan** his executor or **Mrs. Sarah Blackaway** in Charlestown.

All persons indebted to the estate of **John Martin**, late of Pon Pon, deceased, contact **Paul Jenys** who also has recently imported European goods for sale.

Runaway a few days ago from **Othniel Beale**, a Negro girl, named Satyra. Ł3 reward.

Joseph Wragg a parcel of choice Negroes imported in the *Happy Couple*, ----- **Hill**, Master directly from the Coast of Guinea.

All persons indebted to Daniel Laroche & Comp. are desired to pay by December.

Appointed Justices of the Peace for Berkley Co. - **B e n j. Whitaker, James Greme, Daniel Green, Alex Nisbett, James St. John, Charles Cleland, William Wallace**.

Died **Mr. Andrew Allen** on Sept. 6, an eminent merchant of this town, decently buried Monday last (the 8th).

Yesterday arrived here **Capt. Wm. Guttridge**, in 8 weeks from Lisbon.

20 September 1735

On the 23rd at the New Market House will be sold the Sloop *Eagle*, now lying in the harbor. Inquire of **John Parris**.

Just imported in the Ship *Brook* from London and to be sold by **Peter Horry**, women and boys and girls shoes, etc.

To be sold 3 stills, inquire of the printer.

Just imported in the Ship *Brook*, **John Keet**, Commander, and to be sold by **William Roper**,... (long list of goods).

To be sold by **William Harvey**, English or dwarf peas, oats, hay, etc.

To be sold a tract of land on the north side of Ashley River, 800 or 900 acres within a mile of Dorchester Town, being a part of Woodbury Plantation. Inquire of **George Nicholas** at Dorchester Town or **Capt. Rob. Austin**, merchant in Charlestown.

To be let or sold a house with 4 rooms on a floor, with a good kitchen, etc. there being 12 rooms in all with good water and pump, over against **Mr. Jeans**, the Glazer. Inquire of **Tho. Weaver**, carpenter.

27 September 1735

House sign and ship painting and glazing work by **Richard Marten**, two houses down from **Mr. Brand's** in Charlestown.

To be sold 458 acres in Colleton Co. on Combake River bounding to the South by **William Haleman's** land, to the west by land belonging to **Mr. Godfrey**. Inquire of **Peter May** or **Issac Mazyck, Jun.** in Charlestown.

To be sold part of a town lot in Charlestown, #103 fronts 50' on a little street that leads from Ashley River to the broad path and in depth is 100'. It is newly fenced in and the garden planted. Inquire of **Mr. Portail**, Baker, in Elliot's Street.

Runaway on the 4th from Nath. Wickham's Plantation at Winyaw Ferry, 3 Negro fellows named Quaw, Sam, and Caesar, all Sawyers, speak very good English and are sensible fellows (physical descriptions also included). Bring to Nath. Wickham's Plantation near Dorchester to Mr. Allen Well at Winyaw Ferry, or to Wm. Cattell, Jun., Merchant in Charlestown for a 40s reward by Nath. Wickham.

To be sold in the shop formerly kept by Mrs. Owen in Broad Street next door to Mr. Breton all sorts of millinery ware, and all sorts of European goods at reasonable prices by Sarah & Lucy Weaver.

Runaway a milatto fellow named Jack Davis, belonging to Tho. Wright. Bring to Richard or Robert Wright in Charlestown for a Ł5 reward.

Runaway 2 Negro men named Sambo and Tommy lately belonging to Benjamin Godfrey, deceased. They are supposed to be harbored in or near Charlestown. Whoever brings them to their master in Charlestown shall receive a Ł5 reward. Benj. Whitaker.

Goods imported in the *Brook* sold by:
1. John Beswicke next door to Mr. Neri's in Broad St.
2. Wm. Lasserre at his store over against the Court House.
3. John Watson at his store opposite to Elliot's Bridge.

Whereas several persons have been seen taking away marsh mud and shells from the marsh on each side of New Town Creek joining to Ashley River. Notice of intent to prosecute is given by William Bull.

Whereas Thomas Millichamp, charged with counterfeiting, has lately with John Young and two other prisoners also charged with felonies escaped from jail in Charlestown. Ł50 reward offered for his return.

The Schooner *Endeavor*, John Ridley, Master bound for Winyaw.

4 October 1735
Stolen or strayed from the green in Charlestown on the 18th a brown mare, brand Pb. Whoever brings it to the printer or to Mr. Batebeler in Dorchester will receive a Ł3 reward.

Goods sold by **Richard Wigg** at his shop on the Bay next door to **John Allen's**.

To be sold a tract of land containing 210 acres in St. Andrew's Parish joining to **Col. Bull's** lands. Contact **Peter Girardeau** on the said Plantation.

To be sold a plantation on the south side of Ashley River containing 274 good acres of rice land, with a new dwelling house 30x17 with a Dutch roof, 2 barns, within 3 miles of **M r . Thomas Drayton's** landing. Inquire of **Richard Butler** or **Henry Gibbes** in Charlestown.

To be sold a plantation containing 600 acres on the south side of Ashley River being that where **John Cattell** now lives. Inquire of **John Cattell** or **William Cattell, Jr.** in Charlestown.

Brought to jail in Charlestown, a Negro wench belonging to **John Winfield** in Dorchester.

11 October 1735

For London directly, the Brigt. *Mary*, **Wm. Woodrop**, Commander. For freight or passage treat with the Commander at Mr. Elliot's Bridge or with **James Crokatt**.

Brought to jail in Charlestown: a Negro boy named **W i l l** belonging to **Benj. Law** of Wando Neck, Planter, brought per **Wm. Tipworth**.

To be sold a tract of land in Winyaw lying on the south side of Sampit containing 700 acres, treat with **Mr. Henry Bossard** at the Plantation or with **Thomas Walker** being up Wando River on Thomas Island.

To be sold about 20 miles from Charlestown upon the N.W. Branch of Stono River, etc. Inquire of **Richard Wright**.

Notice is given that **Mary Stevenson**, widow of **John Stevenson**, deceased glazer and planter continues the same business; also has two Negro painters to hire out.

William Yeomans advertises for a good carpenter. **Henning and Shuste** advertise good imported flour for sale.

Mrs. Ann Hargrave advertises 500 acres for sale in Granville Co. on the Combee River joining public land.

Bound for Cape Fear, North Carolina, the Sloop *Broughton*, James McDowall, Master. For freight agree with Peter Payne.

On Weds. the 1st of Oct. died Mrs. Dowding, spouse to Mr. Joseph Dowding of St. James Goose Creek, Shop Keeper; she was a person of true virtue to all that knew her, and she died as she lived a good Christian.

18 October 1735

Whereas Joseph Fitch, late of Berkley Co., Planter, deceased. All debtors required to pay within six weeks to his widow, Constant Fitch.

To be sold 2 tracts of land, one on Port Royal Island bounding the land of John Howell and land surveyed for Alexander Mikey. The other tract lying on the south side of Port Royal River bounding to the north on said river and to the west, south, and east on Mackey's Creek, each tract contains 500 acres. Inquire of William Osborn or Charles Pinckney.

To be sold a tract of land on the west side of Pon Pon River containing 2200 acres within a mile of Parker's Ferry. Treat with James Ferguson on said plantation or with John Champneys in Charlestown.

To be sold on the first Weds. in November at the late dwelling house of Dr. David Anderson in Dorchester all the goods of the deceased, dwelling house, Negroes, etc. By Mrs. Anderson.

Binford and Osmond - Merchants.

On the 29th of September a hearing was held before Justice Dale and Henry Gibbes, J.P.'s for Berkley Co. on the petition of Robert Gray for the benefit of poor debtors who were then in the custody of the Provost Marshall.

Yesterday Samuel Underwood was committed to jail for trial on suspicion that he aided and abetted Thomas Millichamp and Joshua Morgan in counterfeiting.

25 October 1735

Runaway on the 17th Sept. from Joseph Williams, carpenter and joyner in Charlestown, an apprentice lad about 17 years old named Henry Toomer, Jr. he had on a brown Duroy and a blue striped holland jacket, a pair of white trousers, he is a slim, pale looking lad and has a mole on the left side of his neck. £5 reward if he is returned to his father **Henry Toomer** at Stono, or to his Master at **Mr.** Cattell's new house in Charlestown.

Christopher Topham of Dorchester, Store Keeper intends to leave this province in April and desires that his accounts be settled.

Hugh Evans enters into partnership this day with **Wilson Wilson** (or **Wilton**).

All persons having any demands on estate of **Sabina Taylor**, late deceased, are desired to bring them within 3 weeks to **Thomas Taylor**, administrator of the estate.

Commissioners of St. Philips Charlestown are enjoined by Act to finish a broad road containing 24 foot and a ditch 4 feet wide at the top from the Quarter House to the broad path lately laid out and finished in St. Andrew's Parish which is 1 1/6 mile in length. Proposals accepted by the Commissioners at the house of **Col. Miles Brewton** in Charlestown on Nov. 5. Commissioners **Miles Brewton, Dan. Green, John Sheppard,** and **John Dart**.

Brought to jail in Charlestown, a Negro boy named **Jack**, says he belongs to **Mr. Westbury** at Pon Pon, taken up by **Samuel Lacy** and another Negro boy taken up by **Alexander Anderson**.

All persons indebted to **Peter Hunter** and **Thomas Conn** are desired to settle their accounts by Dec. 1 as they intend to leave for Great Britain in March.

To be sold a plantation in St. John's Parish on the eastern branch of Cooper River, about 1 1/2 miles from Capt. Bonneau's Ferry, containing 1032 acres. Inquire of **Dr. Jacob Martin** in Charlestown also a parcel of fine slaves for sale at the Plantation.

On Sat. last **Mr. Rowland Serjant** was sent to town in irons in a boat from Port Royal under a strong guard of soldiers, by the order of **Lt. Donegal** of said fort, for having taken the boldness, as **Serjant** alleges, to ask the said Lieutenant for a just debt due to him some time ago. After a hearing before the Governor in Council, and immediately brought charges of battery and false imprisonment against the commanding officer of the Guard and two of his men who were committed to jail, and on Monday gave bail.

My readers will undoubtedly expect to see in this paper an account of the trial of **Joshua Morgan**, but I can only inform them that the petit jury on one indictment (tho the evidence in the case was thought to be very full) found him not guilty, the Counsel for the King thought fit not to proceed in the two other indictments till next sessions when perhaps another jury will think the evidence offered is sufficient to convict, and justice may be done to the public and their country.

In the Court of Common Pleas on Monday a case between **Wm. Gascoyne**, Plaintiff and **John Coit**, defendant for libel in the Gazette at damages of Ł1000. After argument of counsel on both side the jury found for the Plaintiff 5 shillings damage only.

1 November 1735

All persons indebted to **David Allan**, Vintner of Charlestown are desired to pay the same to **Emmanuel Smith**, Taylor of Charlestown by Dec. 6 or will be sued by **Rowland Vaughans**, attorney. By **David Allan**.

All persons indebted to **Anth. Mathews**, late of Charlestown, deceased are desired to pay same by **Anth. Mathews**.

To be sold in the Parish of St. Thomas at **Johnson's** house, sundry goods by Peter Birot & Co. **Mr. Wm. Guianard** advertises as a cooper on Elliot's Bridge, he also has a house for let next to the White Horse, inquire of **Birot** on Elliot's Bridge.

To be sold part of Lot #103, fronts on a little street leading from Ashley River to the broad path 50' and a depth of 110' with a store house thereon. Inquire of **Thomas Visser**, Soap boiler in Union St.

Two hundred acres for sale with a good dwelling house and cellars in the Parish of Christ Church, 4 miles from Charlestown. Inquire of **Jacob Bond**.

To be sold a tract of land containing 370 acres lying on the Indian land to the southward near Port Royal Island. Inquire of **Mrs. Barret** on James Island or **Auth. Mathews** in Charlestown.

To be sold a lot in Dorchester Town fronting the Bay, with a good brick dwelling house 40x30 with 3 rooms on a floor with very good cellars also a wooden store 50x20. Treat with **Gillson Clapp** in Charlestown.

John and **Alexander Rigg,** merchants advertise goods for sale.

Goods imported in the *Queen Elizabeth* from London, **Capt. John Bishop,** Master, sold by **Edward Hext** at his store on the north end of the Bay, also sold by **John Watson** at his store over against Elliot's Bridge and **William Lasserre** at his store over against the Court-house.

8 November 1735
A very good Rhode Island pacing horse to be sold by **M r. Carvalto** in Elliot's Street.

Two thousand acres for sale by **Wm. Weekly** on the north side of Sampit River, a mile fronting the said river. Inquire of **Robert Stewart.**

Rene' Ravenal seeks a tanner and currier. Agree with him at his plantation in St. John's Parish or with **Issac Mazyck, Jun.** in Charlestown.

Wm. Linthwaite sells several brands of snuff.

To be sold by **Marcantoine Besselley** on the Bay, next door to **Gillson Clapp,** lime juice, rum, pig-tail and other tobaccos.

To be sold at the house of **Capt. Gerret Vanvelsen** in Charlestown, 12 young Negro men, and a young Negro wench.

A parcel of choice slaves to be sold on the 19th at the house where **Mrs. Elizabeth Hill** now lives, about a mile from Charlestown.

Because of his unexpected illness the sale of slaves by **D r. Jacob Martin** fixed upon the 26 of November, is cancelled indefinitely.

The inhabitants of the town increasing every day, the two companies of foot soldiers have been divided into four, whereas **Capt. Adam Beauchamp** has the first, **Mr. Joseph Massey** was appointed Captain of the second, **Mr. William Pinckney**, Captain of the third and **Mr. Childermas Croft**, Captain of the fourth.

Last Thursday **Mr. Issac Chardon**, a very worthy eminent merchant of this town was married to **Mary Woodward** of James Island, a young lady of conspicuous merit and a large fortune.

John Johnson – searcher to his Majesty's Custom house.

On the 26th arrived here **Capt. John Stuart**, master of the Ship *Ogle* from Antigua with 52 Spaniards on board that he rescued with great risk from a ship in distress, he having only 12 hands aboard.

15 November 1735

Goods imported by the Ship *Charles*, from London, **James Reid**, Master to be sold by **James Reid** at **Richard Hill's** on the Bay.

At the Courtroom, a Ball, on Monday the 15th of December to begin precisely at 5:00. **Henry Holt**, Master.

Thomas Walker, who lives about 6 miles from Charlestown at Wando River sells pine timber.

James Smallwood advertises European goods for sale on the Bay. Also desires that all his debts be paid as he intends to leave shopkeeping this winter. He also asks that those indebted to the estate of **Mr. Benj. Godfrey** pay him for **Godfrey's** debts.

Runaway on the 3rd of November from **Thomas Heyward** of James Island, a young Negro wench named **Amy**, country born, she is very black, has thick lips and large breasts, had on a Oznabrig coat and jacket, and an old Negro cloth gown.

All persons indebted to **Peter Hunter** and **Tho. Conn** are desired to pay by the 1st of March as **Hunter** desires to leave the partnership and go to Great Britain.

Brought to jail in Charlestown a Negro fellow, name unknown, taken up by **Henry Wood**.

22 November 1735

All persons indebted to **Wm. McKenzie** are desired to pay their debts by the 1st of Feb. or be sued by **Charles Pinckney.**

To be sold, a plantation called Hampstead, 5 miles from Charlestown with a good dwelling house thereon, a large garden, an avenue of orange trees, an orchard with quince apples, peach and nectarine trees the whole plantation under cedar and rail fence. Treat with **Mr. John Chevilles** at the Plantation or **Mr. Wm. Lassere's** in town.

Peter Horry advertises goods for sale just imported in the *Whitfield* Brigantine from Bristol.

The gentlemen of Port Royal propose to show 21 cocks against the whole province to take place in one month for £20 a battle, and £100 for odd battle. Whoever is inclined to enter the lists contact **Tho. Ellery** in Charlestown.

To the Gentleman of Port Royal, there is at the house of **M r. Charles Shepheard** a mussled cock, named Bougre de Sot who will fight against any cock in this province, give or take an ounce, for £100 currency. Whoever has the punk to take up the aforesaid Bougre de Sot, treat with **Charles Shepheard** for time and place.

The anniversary meeting of the St. Andrew's Club will be held on the 1st day of December at the house of **Mr. Charles Shepheard**, Vintner in Charlestown. By **James Michie,** secretary.

29 November 1735

Mr. Scott (who married **Col. Fenwicke's** daughter) went with the Yachts to fetch the King from Helvoetsburys, and is to have a 20 gun ship on his return.

James Wright received a commission for the Offices of Remembrance, Clerk of the Pleas and Entreats of the Court of Exchequer.

To be sold a 3rd part of a town lot on Broad Street known in the model of the town plot by #15. Inquire of **Eliz. Story** in Charlestown.

John Beswicke in Charlestown asks that all debts owed to estate of David Anderson, deceased, be paid.

Charlest Perroneau and Comp. will sell at public auction at the store at Bear Bluff all goods, merchandise, houses, lands, and slaves belonging to the company.

Reading, writing and arithmetic to be taught by Edward Clark at the house of Mrs. Lydia Viart near the new intended market.

Goods imported in the Ship *Catherine*, to be sold cheap as usual, by Wm. Stone who is removed from White Point to Col. Hext's new house in Tradd St.

Goods imported in Capt. Baker, and to be sold by Jonathan Scott at Thomas Lloyd's on the Bay.

To be sold by Marcantoine Besselley on the Bay, next door to Mr. Gillson Clapp, very good lime juice, rum, pig-tail and other tobacco.

Goods imported in the Snow *Angelie*, John Hay, Master from Leith & Madeira and to be sold by Crokatt & Seaman at their store in Broad St.

Stolen out of a garden near the Church in Charlestown on Thursday the 20th, a slim bay mare, with a switch tail, about 7 years old, etc. Reward offered by Christopher Worsted.

Imported in the *John & Mary*, John Payne directly from London and to be sold by Wm. Ramsey & Co. at their store at George Town Winyaw (large assortment of goods).

Goods imported in the Ship *Catherine*, Capt. Toy (cloth items) to be sold by Cleland & Wallace at the Widow Kings in Broad St.

Goods imported in the *Neptune*, Pink, Capt. Graham from Bristol to be sold by Benjamin Savage & Co.; goods very reasonably priced, he desiring to go off this Province early in the Spring.

Goods imported in the *Bogdon*, J. Jones, Master from Bristol, and to be sold by John McKenzie at his store opposite to Mr. Wm. McKenzie.

6 December 1735

Brought to jail at Charlestown, a Negro fellow taken up at Peter Hume's Plantation.

Goods to be sold by Thomas Thompson at the store of Wm. Kellaway in Broad St.

To be sold 313 acres upon Ashley Ferry joining Mr. Daniel Cartwright's. Treat with Josiah Baker.

Stolen or strayed out of Mrs. Dawe's pasture near Charlestown, a large white mare, 6 years old, etc. reward offered. Any person seeking employment as an overseer, and can be well recommended, may speak with J. Vicaridge who proposes to settle a Plantation the first of February next at Winyaw on Black River with 20 Negroes to make turpentine, tar and pitch. He may be spoken to at Mrs. Dawe's or at his own Plantation on Cooper River in St. Thomas Parish.

Daniel Badger lately arrived from Boston does house and ship painting. He may be heard of at Mr. Warham's, Joiner in Tradd St.

Robert Pringle advertises goods for sale at the House lately possessed by Messrs. Jenys & Baker on the Bay.

13 December 1735

Goods sold in Thomas Elliot's Alley by Thomas Gates.

A plantation containing 730 acres about 12 miles from Charlestown for sale. Inquire of John Laurens, Sadler in Charlestown.

Mr. Whitaker wishes to buy 2 or 3 horses suitable for draught.

Any gentleman interested in joining the society for the Mutual Insurance of their houses against fire are desired to meet at the house of Capt. William Pinckney on the Bay on Tuesday at 5:00 in the afternoon.

Whereas Joseph Fitch, late of Berkley County, planter deceased, made a will some time before his death. All debtors and creditors as well as those of Manley Williamson, late of Ashley River Planter deceased are to settle with Constant

141

Fitch, the widow of Joseph at her plantation near Ashley Ferry.

An overseer that understands plantations is desired by Mr. Lake at his Plantation on Ashley River, that formerly belonged to Mr. Godfrey. Inquire there or at William Yeoman's in Charlestown.

Anthony Corne, brazier, lately from London, is living in Elliot's St. where he does business.

To be sold by Mr. Priber near Mr. Laurans, the Sadler, clothes, etc.

Two Runaway Negro men, one a tall elderly fellow named Guam, a taylor by trade, the other a short, thick fellow named Steven was Patron of Mr. Vander Dussen's wood perriauger. If located bring to jail or to Al. Vander Dussen.

All persons indebted to Anthony and James Mathews and Co. are desired to pay.

Tickets for a vocal concert at the Council Chamber on Friday at 6:00 may be obtained at Mr. Cook's house.

Vacancy for an overseer, apply with Mr. Thomas Cheesmann at his Plantation in Goose Creek.

20 December 1735
The printer, L. Timothy corrects an article appearing on Oct. 25 concerning Lt. Delagal and Mr. Rowland Serjean.

To be sold a plantation on Wando Neck containing 355 acres, fronting the River, about 16 miles by water from Charlestown. Contact Samuel Bullock, living on the said Wando Neck.

Run Away from Alexander Frissel in Christ Church Parish, a Negro man of a yellow color named Casar, branded on the left thigh A. F., wearing a white cotton gown, he is well set.

Brought to jail in Charlestown a Negro Boy named Cyrus. Taken up at Pon Pon per Bert Rogers.

Whereas in October last a bay gelding branded on the mounting shoulder WD, with three white feet and a white face, was purchased by my traders for £40 worth of goods in Oconey

Town in the Cherokee nation from an Indian man belonging to Keyokee which horse is at my Plantation called Exeter, in the Parish of St. John's. Whoever has a claim on said horse may apply there to **Hugh Butler**.

To be let, a convenient brick dwelling house, with several out houses with a good landing. It is within one mile of Dorchester Town on the north side of Ashley River. Contact **Daniel Pepper** at the said house.

27 December 1735

To be sold a tract of land on the north side of Ashley River containing 800-900 acres within a mile of Dorchester being part of Woodbury Plantation, the front being high bluff land. Contact **George Nicholas** at Dorchester or **Capt. Rob. Austin,** merchant in Charlestown.

A young heifer of white color and about 3 years of age, was strayed and kept along with my cattle now 12 months. Whoever owns her should contact **John Combe'** at the Orange Quarters.

BATEFELLOW, Thomas 43
BATEMAN, Titus 117
BATTIN, Adam 26 52 53 Alan 38
BAXTER, Ja 124
BAYLER, Thomas 88
BAYLEY, John 45
BAYLY, John 24 Tong 78
BEACH, Richard 55
BEAK, Capt 66
BEAL, Capt 86
BEALE, Hoffneil 73 Oth 117 Othniel 68 115 126 130 William 88
BEALL, Mr 78
BEALS, Othnieo 69
BEARMAN, Christoph 124
BEATON, Stephen 6
BEAUCHAMP, Adam 6 9 62 92 93 138
BECKMAN, Mary 20 Titus 20
BEDON, Henry 24 42 53 55 85 Richard 72 Steph 123 Stephen 62 95 97
BEE, Capt 17 John 12 26 50 79 John Jr 33 41 71 John Sr 41 72
BEGGON, Justin 72
BELL, Dan 15 Mrs 13 Wm 123
BELLAMY, Sally 10
BELLINGER, Edmund 73 78 Edward 71
BELLINGERS, Edmund 117
BELTYSON, Jonath 123
BENN, Moses 94
BENNELL, John 79
BENNET, Moses 6
BENNISON, Geo 115 124
BENOITT, Peter 124
BERESFORD, John 84 Mr 20
BERNARD, Mr 109
BERNER, John 91
BERTSON, William 4
BESSELLEY, Marcantoine 137 140
BESTOY, Alexander 72
BESWICKE, John 132 140
BETTERSON, Mary 90
BETTISOM, Catherine 44
BINFORD, 134 Mr 33 Thomas 2 56
BIRET, Peter 70
BIROT, Mr 114 Peter 84 95 101 136

BISBY, Wm 113
BISHOP, John 69 137
BLACKAWAY, Sarah 130
BLADES, John 79-81
BLAKE, Col 85 124 Joseph 73
BLAKELY, John 117
BLAKEWAY, Sarah 109
BLAND, Richard 115 124
BLONDEL, Mr 63
BLYTH, Th 112
BLYTHE, 15 Tho 124
BODERT, Is 124
BODYCOAT, Mr 91
BOLEM, Thomas 91
BOLEN, Thomas 118
BOLLING, Thomas 44
BOLTON, Thomas 10 31 79 99 118
BOND, Jacob 73 97 98 110 136 Thomas 66
BONIN, J 124
BONNEAU, Anthony 73 Anthony Jr 71
BOON, Eliz 6
BOONE, Anne 40 J 64 Joseph 72 73 Th 112 Tho 124 Thomas 40 73
BOSHER, Tho 124
BOSSARD, Henry 16 133
BOURGET, Dan 24 Daniel 19 101
BOURNEAU, Anth 65 Jacob 98
BOVET, John Peter 28
BOYAURDS, Mr 61
BRADFORD, William 72 Wm 113
BRAILEFORD, John 32
BRAND, John 55 Mr 131
BRANDE, Mr 37
BRANDIN, S 2
BRANDT, Mr 8 45
BRANFORD, Mr 119
BRASLEUR, Francis le 90
BRASSEUR, Fr le 126 Fran le 61 116 Francis le 22 37 102
BRASSEURS, Mr 90
BRASSEURT, Fr le 110
BRAUGHTON, Hon Col 9 Nathanial 9
BREASSEUR, Fr le 66
BREBANT, Daniel 33
BRECKINGTON, Wm 124
BRESSEUR, Fr le 108
BRETON, Dr 48 John 40 44 66 Mr

BRETON (continued)
47 90 132
BREUTON, Robert 68
BREWELL, William 72
BREWTON, Capt 49 118 Col 8
Mary 43 Miles 3 41 50 65 112
120 126 135 Robert 9 73 98
BRIMBAT, Paul 72
BRISLEY, Susanna 106
BROKE, Robert 44
BROOMHEAD, 15
BROUGHTON, Christiana 1 Hon
Col 1 51 Nath 118 Nathaniel 73
124 Thomas 72
BROWDEN, Andrew 73
BROWN, John 45 47 Mathew 40
Matthew 67 Mr 13 Thomas 72
Walter 16 William 14
BRUCE, John 11 83
BRUNNEAU, Henry 32
BRUNSONS, Mr 128
BRYAN, Hugh 102 103 Jo 113
John 62 Jonath 123 Joseph 102
103 Mrs 67
BUCHANAN, John 24 Robert 5
William 102
BULL, Col 15 133 William 45
126 132 Wm 124
BULLARD, Edw 124 Edward 100
115 Griffith 98 115
BULLIME, Tho 129
BULLIN, Thomas 54
BULLOCH, Ja 122
BULLOCK, James 19 65 Jane 72
Samuel 120 142
BURCHERS, William Elvis 79
BURLEY, Charles 13
BURLY, Hanna 113
BURN, Francis 60
BURNET, Edward 90
BURNHAM, Charles 4 42 91 Mrs
65
BURNLY, Hannah 124
BUSTON, Th 124
BUTLER, Hugh 21 91 105 143
Joseph 128 Richard 133 Tho 32
123 Thomas 48 72 76
BUTTLER, Thomas 83
BYDON, John 96
BYNFORD, 113
CAAN, John 71 Thomas 71
CALVAT, Peter 96

CALVETT, Peter 113
CAMERON, John 23
CAMPBELL, Henry 12 Hugh 88
112
CANTEY, William 5
CAPERS, Rich 112 124 Richard
103 Thomas 103
CARMICHAEL, J 123 John 36
CARNEY, Peter 69
CARPENTER, Mary 6
CARRUTHERS, John 27 127
CARTWRIGHT, Daniel 11 64 65
116 141 Richard 116
CARVALIS, 130
CARVALLO, Mr 79 109
CARVALTO, Mr 137
CARWITHEN, Mrs 114 William
46 74 114 Wm 124
CARWITHERS, Mr 130
CASHPULL, Susanna 106 William 106
CATTELL, 82 Anne 10 Cath 101
Catherine 4 48 84 John 71 133
Mr 135 Peter 48 William 5 10
23 43 69 71 73 84 86 William
Jr 4 24 33 44 133 Wm 48 Wm
Jr 132
CAUSTON, Thomas 77 78
CAWOOD, Thomas 84
CHAMBERLAIN, Sarah 124
CHAMBERS, Joseph 46 74
CHAMPLY, John 4
CHAMPNEY, John 3 101
CHAMPNEYS, John 25 46 48 110
115 117 134
CHAPMAN, Will 4
CHARDON, Is 124 Issac 17 26 28
60 61 81 85 90 100 118 128 138
Laroche 90 Mary 138 Mr 44
117 Winyaw 128
CHASSEREAU, Peter 95
CHEATHAM, William 3 48
CHEESMAN, Thomas 109
CHEESMANN, Thomas 142
CHETHAM, William 25
CHEVELIET, John 98
CHEVILLES, John 139
CHICKEN, George 106
CHIDLEY, Henry 31
CHIESELLE, Mr 87
CHILD, Benj 122 Isaac 4 Mr 18
CHRISTIAN, Benjamin 48

CHRISTIE, Thomas 78
CLAPP, Gilison 4 26 Gillison 73
  Gillson 55 120 137 140
CLARK, Edward 140
CLAY, William 87
CLEILAND, Wm 43
CLELAND, 109 112 113 140
  Charles 130 John 119 Mary 119
CLELLAND, William 9
CLEWS, William 70
CLIFFORD, J 7 Mr 3 Tho 11 123
  124 Thomas 41 51 64 72 87
  103
CLIFORD, Tho 113
CLIN, Frank 63
CLOY, Mr 110
CLUMTREE, 76
COACHMEN, John 72
COAT, William 72
COBRIE, Mr 9
COCHRAN, Ja 112 James 14 55
  108 124 John 124 Mary 14 Wm
  122
COCKRAN, James 89
CODNER, Charles 68
CODNOR, Mr 7
COIT, John 107 136
COITE, Mr 104
COKE, Benthy 124
COLCOCK, John 20
COLE, Thomas 6
COLEBATCH, George 114
COLEMAN, John 33
COLETON, John 73 Mr 85
COLLETON, 32 Elizabeth 106
  George 106 John 3 105 125
COLLIER, Tho 124
COLLINS, Jonah 73 Mrs 69
COLLIS, Robert 102
COLT, Wm 108
COMBE, John 111 143 Mrs 111
COMMANDER, Saml 124
COMPTON, Capt 77
CONN, Tho 138 Thomas 135
CONNER, John 75
CONNETTE, John 27
CONSEE, Benjamin de la 73
COOK, J 124 Mr 142 Mrs 18
COOKE, Giles 3
COOKS, Mrs 36
COOPER, Dr 45 77 80 Mr 78 102
  Robert 109 Tho 123 Thomas 10

COOPER (continued)
  21 45 76 77 85 111 Wm 115 124
COOTE, William 53
CORBETT, Thomas 102
CORDES, Thomas 73
CORNE, Anthony 142
CORNUCK, John 38
COUNSEIRE, Benj Dela 124
COX, Ezek 124 Ezekiel 112
CRAWFORD, Dan 122 Daniel 43
  49 51 60 68 69 96 99 David 43
  Hugh 70 Mr 10 Sally 10
CRAWL, Wm 124
CRIPS, Wm 113
CROFT, Abraham 67 Childerman
  67 Childermas 24 138 Edw 67
  112 Edward 66 120 Mr 83
  Rebecca 47
CROKAT, James 61
CROKATT, 140 James 4 17 21 25
  26 34 37 43 77 86 103 116 133
  John 85 Mr 86 117
CROLL, Tho 115
CROSS, Capt 62 Ed 3 Hill 3 22
  Mrs 10
CROXSON, Elizabeth 6
CRRIGH, Samuel 71
CUMESTOCK, Peter 88
D'HARRIRTTE, Benjamin 68
DALE, Dr 45 Justice 134 Thomas
  43 66 68 73 126 127
DALTON, Ja 124 James 74 81
DANDRIDGE, Francis 83
DANIEL, Govenor 71 John 7 11 16
  20 68 73 81 89 90 97 130
DANIELS, John 103
DART, John 15 41 50 56 82 106
  107 135
DAVIDS, Issac 124
DAVIES, David 17
DAVIS, Capt 54 David 32 Jack
  132 Mr 37 Pen 80 Roger 50
  William 48
DAW, Mrs 108
DAWBURR, Henry 88
DAWE, Mrs 141
DE'VEAUX, James 5
DEAN, Dan 122
DEANE, Daniel 39
DEARSLEY, Richard 84
DEDCOTT, Eliz 123 Elizabeth 71
DELAGAL, Lt 142

DELAMARE, Mrs 100
DELAVILLETTE, Andr 124
DELEMORE, John 112 Katherine 112
DELORI, Joseph 76
DEMBSTER, Gregory 75
DENNIS, Benj 60 Benjamin 24 Ladling 76 Laurence 4 Lawrence 35
DERBY, John 89 Michael 73
DETMAR, Albert 17 109
DEVEAUX, James 93
DEVYERO, Patrick 39
DICK, Geo 112
DICKES, Arthur 116
DICKSON, Tho 112
DIDCOTT, Joseph 22
DILL, Elizabeth 48
DILLION, Garrat 32
DINGO, Joseph 72
DISTON, Thomas 111
DOBREE, Elias 78 Elisha 78
DOMMING, Mr 15
DONEGAL, Lt 135
DONNING, Capt 52 Thomas 118 William 5 27 118 Wm 124
DOPSON, Joseph 117
DORMOUNT, Barth 117
DOUGLAS, Capt 23 James 25
DOURSAINT, Mr 70
DOWDING, Joseph 134 Mrs 134
DRAKE, Jonathan 112 Mary 124 Samuel 4 112
DRAYDON, Thomas 73
DRAYTON, Ann 100 Anne 36 Mr 82 Mrs 100 T 32 Thomas 133
DRIVE, William 73
DRY, Mr 18 61 84 111 122 Will 7 William 41 54 55 Wm 123
DRYE, Mr 72
DUBOIT, Abraham 31
DUBOSE, Ja 124
DUBUC, Abraham 39
DUCAT, George 8 42 59 66
DUCHE, Andrew 106
DUMABE, James 32
DUNCAN, Thomas 81 93
DUPOISDON, Mrs 22
DUPONT, Abr 124
DUPRE, Corn 112
DUPREE, Corn 124
DURAND, Levi 24

DURANQUE, J 115
DURANT, Hen 113
DURHAM, David 4
DWANT, Henry 124
DWIGHT, Christiana 1 Rev Mr 1
DYER, Stephen 99
DYSON, Edw 25
EAGLE, Richard 5 7 14
EAGLES, Richard 34 79 119 127
EDGHILL, Richard 14
EDWARDS, Ed 112 Mr 122 Uriah 52
EGLIN, John 127
ELDRIDGE, Jane 97 Mrs 38 60 S 11
ELLERY, Mr 38 111 Tho 24 26 105 139 Thomas 10 13 24 36 39 64 91 93 102 125
ELLIOT, Ann 92 John 40 Joseph 82 Mr 91 Mrs 21 Th 113 Tho 123 Thomas 6 9 65 87 Wilham 64 William Jr 105 Wm 128
ELLIOTT, 47 52 Anne 42 72 T 15 Tho 48 Thomas 14 40 68 72 Thomas Sr 75 William 68 William Jr 73
ELLIS, Mr 7
EMMERSON, George 115
ENMS, Hezekiah 48 William 48
ESCOT, Gabriel 79
ESCOTT, 10 86 89 Capt 107 Gabr 81 Gabriel 109 115 120 Mr 120
ESSEX, Mr Jr 87
ETHERITLGE, Tho 2
EVANS, Hugh 1 27 53 63 79-81 83 87 114 135 Mr 10
EVELEIGH, Mr 11 Sam 28 110 Samuel 16 35 38 53 73 107
EVERLEIGH, Samuel 20 95
EVERSON, Thomas 71 115
FAIRCHILD, Eliz 121 John 31 102 128 Mr 83 Thomas 31 51 102 Wm 124 128
FAIRLESS, Tho 125
FARLESS, Thomas 41
FARLEY, George 72
FARLY, George 71
FARR, John 37 Tho 51 124 Thomas 40 114
FARREL, Brent 53
FARRINGTON, Ensign 63
FASOIN, Elias 124

FENDIN, J 124
FENIWICKE, John 37
FENWICK, John 9
FENWICKE, Col 38 John 45 59
  99 126 Mr 139
FERGUSON, Henry 115 Ja 113
  James 72 110 117 134 Js 123
  Mr 77 Tho 115 Thomas 74
FIDLER, Jos 124
FIDLINGS, John 74
FIELD, 76 Thomas 74
FINCH, Capt 127
FINLEY, Richard 73
FINWICK, John 68 72
FISHER, James 24 34 John 3
FITCH, Constant 134 141 142
  Joseph 134 141 142 Tob 125
  Tobias 5 73 129
FITZGERALD, Gerald 56
FLAVEL, Mrs 120
FLAVELL, Rebecca 113
FLAVELS, Mrs 99
FLEDGER, Robert 115
FLEMING, Thomas 12 40 42 56
  65 90
FLEMMING, Tho 129 Thomas 78
FLETCHER, Henry 54
FLEY, Samuel 114
FLOWER, Henry 86 Joseph Ed-
  ward 90
FLOWERS, Joseph Edward 28
FLUD, J 112
FLY, Samuel 95
FOGARTY, John 122
FOISLIN, Elias Jr 73
FOISSIN, Elias 122
FORBESS, Hugh 75
FORD, Nathanial 33 Nathaniel 55
  Simon 53 Stephen 12 40 71
  Thomas 71 William 61
FORESTER, Lord 21 39
FORREST, Henry 89
FORRESTER, Charles 42
FORSTER, Arthur 65 Richard 93
FOTHERGILL, Richard 117
FOWLER, James 14 22 45 John
  127 Mr 61 80
FOX, Joseph 23 66 74 Justice 92
FRANCIS, Elizabeth 51
FRANKLIN, John 84 85 Richard
  80
FRASER, John 25 49 84

FRAZIER, J 75 John 8 20
FREEMAN, Richard 96
FRENCH, Mr 70 Peter 5
FRISSEL, Alexander 142
FRY, Capt 63 65 Joseph 88
FUBBER, Francis 89
FULLER, 116 Richard 73 86 Wil-
  liam 64 119 William Jr 73
  Wm 31
FULLERTON, Rev Mr 129
FULTON, David 124
FURGUSON, Ja 124 Tho 124 Wil-
  liam 8 Wm 124
GADSDEN, Capt 102 Tho 101
  Thomas 41 85 129
GADSTON, Capt 71 74 Thomas 72
  73
GALE, Hannah 66 Mrs 31 117 129
GARDEN, A 31
GARNIER, Jos 124
GASCOIGN, Capt 41
GASCOIGNE, Capt 61 John 20 62
GASCOIN, William 66
GASCOYNE, Wm 104 107 136
GATES, Mr 20 Thomas 46 77 84
  101 104 141
GERMAN, Ralph 84
GIBBEN, Joseph 88
GIBBES, Henry 24 133 134 Wm
  28
GIBBON, Daniel 12
GIBBS, Henry 49 73 John 73
GIBSON, Daniel 32 36 Dr 15 24 26
  44 Wm 127 128
GIGNILLEAT, Mr 26
GIGNILLIAT, Henry 16 25 Mr 64
  84
GIGNILLIOT, Henry 81
GIGNILLOT, Mr 23
GILBERT, Edward 31 39
GILL, Mullarrey 44
GINARDEAN, Peter 124
GIRARDEAU, Peter 8 133
GITTENS, John 49
GIUTTERES, 130
GLAZE, Mal 59 67 Malachi 20 86
  Malachia 38 99 Malachy 71 73
  Mr 128
GLAZER, Samuel 114
GLEN, William 85
GLOVER, Col 38 Mr 86 William
  113

GODDIN, Benjamin 73
GODFREY, Benj 105 138 Ben-
jamin 4 23 69 103 119 132
John 2 6 Mr 131 142 Rich 124
GODIN, 56 Benjamin 14 27 86 Mr
81 Mrs 45
GODLIN, Benj 127
GODSDEN, Thomas 124
GODSEN, Thomas 26
GOFFE, Roger 39
GOLDEN, Benjamin 75
GOLIGHTLY, Culcheth 70
GOODBEE, Alexander 11 James
11
GOODBY, Alex 90
GOODING, Mr 125
GOODMAN, Thomas 61 80
GOODRIDGE, Thomas 88
GOODWIN, Richard 92 116
GORDON, Capt 109 James 101
William 52
GOUDET, Mr 12
GOUGH, John 33 124 Mr 2
GOUIRAN, Charlotte 33 Mr 4
GRAHAM, Abr 123 124 Abraham
55 Capt 140
GRANES, James 4
GRAY, J 124 Robert 134 William
67 Wm 113
GREELAND, William 71
GREEME, James 38 49 76
GREEN, Capt 70 129 Dan 123 135
Daniel 35 55 130 Elizabeth 55
J 115 John 72 124
GREENE, Daniel 37 86 92 120
GREENLAND, Wm 124
GREGORY, J 115 John 124 T
Neophilus 26 Tileophious 73
GREIG, Charles 88 89
GREME, James 21 25 26 45 47 53
55 67 119 130 Mr 45
GRENIER, Mrs 114
GREY, Samuel 51
GRIFFEN, Tho 25
GRIFFIN, Capt 23
GRIMBALL, Paul 67
GRIMKE, 85 92 103
GRIMSTONE, Mr 78
GRONAN, Mr 65
GROVE, Elizabeth 108 John 108
Sarah 108 William 108
GRUNBAL, Is 123

GUERARD, 56 John 14 27
GUERERD, John 75
GUERNIER, John 16
GUIANARD, Wm 136
GUILD, Thomas 88
GUILLAIRD, Pet 33
GUTERES, Mr 109
GUTTERES, Mr 79
GUTTRIDGE, Wm 131
GUY, Rev Mr 10
GUYLE, Madame 74
HADDRELL, Geo 84 George 77
HAIMES, Nicholas 13
HAINES, Nicholas 22 56
HALE, Robert 97
HALEM, Richard 76
HALEMAN, William 131
HALL, Andrew 50 Arthur 4 8
Charles 73 George 36 Mary 8
Richard 70 Rob 109 Robert 83
Thomas 129
HAMERTON, John 27 45 Mrs 38
47
HAMILTON, John 32 Paul 5 124
William 126 Wm 114
HAMLEN, John 72
HAMMER, John 72
HAMMERTON, J 122 John 9 107
109 Mr Secretary 15 Mrs 11 82
William 9 11
HANDLEN, Thomas 71
HANDLIN, J 113
HANKING, Thomas 62
HANNAH, James 96
HANSCOMB, Aaron 113
HANSCOURT, Jos 113
HANSER, William 52
HARGRAVE, Ann 133 Charles 3
Henry 14
HARLSTON, Mr 128
HARRIS, Capt 130 Fr 112 124
Hannah 16 20 John 124 Mrs
125 Nick 54 Richard 16 20
HARRISON, John 89
HART, Charles 103 119
HARVEY, Mary 17 Mr 110 Wil-
liam 11 52 131 Wm 113
HARVY, Morris 14
HASELL, James 82 Tho 113
HASKINS, Benjamin 14
HATELL, James 73
HATTON, Capt 52 82 Tho 120

HAVEN, Stephen 34
HAWE, Charles 63
HAY, John 140
HAYDEN, Mrs 31
HAYDON, Mrs 34 35
HAYES, Charles 32
HAYNES, 5 Joseph 6 Mr 68 78 98
   Nich 124 Nicholas 5
HAYS, Charles 33
HAYWARD, Thomas 35
HAZZARD, Wm Jr 124
HEAD, George 75
HEARN, J 112
HEBERT, John 87
HEMMING, Thomas 88
HENDLIN, Eliz 112
HENDRICK, Wm 124
HENLEY, Francis 117
HENNESEY, Capt 85
HENNING, 133 Anne 43 Mrs 47
   Phillippele 100 Tho 37 42
   Thomas 43 85
HERBERT, John 1 43 51
HEUMES, Mr 78
HEWITT, James 54
HEXT, Al 109 Alexander 126 Col
   140 David 69 Edward 26 137
   Hugh 12 Peter Francis 76
   Richard 65
HEYDEN, Gerrat Vander 86
HEYMES, Don Francisco de 76
HEYWARD, Tho 7 Thomas 34 46
   101 110 138
HICKINS, Joseph 14
HICKS, Mathew 27
HIDERWICK, Patrick 127 128
HIGGS, John 88
HILL, 130 Charles 4 21 43 61 72
   82 Elizabeth 85 100 124 137
   John 11 Miss 21 Mr 90 Mrs
   114 Richard 21 43 44 48 56 59
   65 82 85 93 99 105 122 124 127
   129 138 William 88
HILTON, William 89
HIRST, John 43 Sarah 43
HIXTS, Mr 6
HOARD, Experience 115
HODDY, John 124
HOGG, Mrs 50
HOLDEN, Edward 93
HOLEMARK, Tho 54
HOLIDAY, Giles 116

HOLLAND, Edward 20
HOLLIDAY, Giles 119
HOLMAN, Thomas 51 William 72
HOLMES, Is 124 Issac 66 97 103
   Sam 127 Samuel 53 59 60 84
   100 101 120 Thomas 79 83
   Will 124 William 52 Wm 113
HOLSON, Widow 13
HOLT, Henry 86 87 138
HOLTON, T 15
HOLYDAY, Charles 21
HOPKINS, Ja 122
HORRY, Dan 124 Elias 21 71
   Pete 62 Peter 33 60 86 131 139
HOW, Rob 113
HOWARD, Mrs 61 Peter 63 Tho 4
HOWELL, John 91 130 134
HOWES, Job 7 124
HUDSON, Capt 103
HUFT, Thomas 71
HUGER, Daniel 73
HUGHES, Meredith 124
HUGHS, Meredith 66
HUGOE, Bastian 41
HUME, Mr 10 20 Peter 141 Robert
   13 22 28 42 Sophia 49 81 103
   114
HUMES, Robert 93
HUNTER, John 107 Mr 104 Peter
   135 138
HUSBAND, James 77
HUTCHINSON, 85 92 103 Rib 120
   Ribton 4 18 22 52 57 74 92
   Ripton 73 76 Wm 63
HUTCHISON, Charlotte 123
HY---, Henry 65
HYRNE, Henry 117
INDIAN, Betty 82 Deborah 22
   King Tomo Chi Chi 51 Sarah
   40
IRELAND, Richard 10
IZARD, Richard 86
IZORD, Ralph 72 Walter 73
JACKSON, Henry 124
JAMES, Charles 1 Michael 13
JANDON, Dan 124 Dan Jr 124
JANVIER, Lewis 93 118
JARRARD, Christopher 32
JAUDON, Daniel 78
JEANES, Michael 82
JEANS, Mr 131
JEARD, Walter 73

LINING, John 54 62 86
LINKLEY, Christopher 32
LINTHWAIT, Wm 56
LINTHWAITE, William 3 Wm 34
   98 109 137
LIONS, Elizabeth 125
LITTLE, Edward 46 49 50
LIVINGSTON, Henry 68 94 101
   William 14 105 116
LLOYD, Capt 38 47 72 86 James
   22 23 25 John 10 56 99 Mr 34
   87 Th 110 Tho 37 80 Thomas
   43 89 91 140
LLOYDS, Thomas 64
LLYLE, Nicholas 80 81
LOAN, Richard 96
LOGAN, Alex 105 Geo 98 George
   16 19 61 73 97 109 130 Martha
   20
LONG, John 125
LOPTON, John 72
LORD, Joseph 121
LORMIER, Lewis 62 82
LORMIEUR, Mrs 100
LORRY, Anne 119 Thomas 112
LORY, Mrs 86
LOVELACE, Thomas 5
LOVETT, Mary 6 Philip 6
LOVEY, Anne 25
LOW, James 81
LOWLE, Calet 3
LOWNDES, C 97 125 Cha 123
   Charles 129 Robert 96
LOWNDS, Charles 33 Roger 80
LUCAS, Col 86
LUDLAM, Rev Mr 3
LUSK, James 88 114
MACHONE, James 11
MACKENZIE, John 43 William 7
MACKEWN, James 49
MACKEY, Alexander 130 J 115
   Joseph 24 46 59 111
MACNAMAR, Michael 48
MACNAMARA, Michael 36 Mrs
   Christian 36
MACOY, Deborah 87
MAGGEE, Rebecca 118 Wm 118
MAIN, Jonathain 33 Jonathan 26
   42
MALCOLME, John 120
MANIGAULT, Gabriel 42 68 106
   129

MANIGOLT, Gabriel 73
MARETT, Bernard 12 Philip 81
MARION, Gabriel 81
MARRIT, Tho 112
MARTEN, Richard 131
MARTIN, Ja 125 Jacob 135 137
   John 130
MARTINE, Dr 128
MARTYN, Samuel 3
MASON, John 41
MASSEY, Benj 102 Benjamin 33
   Capt 63 101 Edward 27 109
   Joseph 10 36 42 65 102 138
MASSY, Joseph 37
MATHEW, Anth Sr 125
MATHEWS, Anth 136 Anthony
   127 142 Auth 137 Ja 122
   James 33 102 110 142 John 45
   Mr 20
MATTHEWS, Capt 54 Wm 63
MATTHILION, Nicholas 90
MATTHISEN, Nich 102
MATTYSON, Nicholas 72
MAY, Peter 115 125 131
MAYANT, Susannah 125
MAYRANT, Madam 71 Susannah
   125
MAZYCK, Isaac Jr 2 Issac 73 114
   Issac Jr 68 73 120 131 137 Is-
   sac Sr 7 26 35 92 Mrs 7 Paul
   59 71
MAZYK, Is Sr 102 Issac 102 Is-
   sac Jr 81
MCBEAN, Locklin 24
MCCLELLAN, James 36
MCCLELVEY, James 114
MCCLURE, William 71
MCCOLUME, Mr 20
MCDOWALL, James 134
MCDOWELL, James 75
MCELROY, Alex 125
MCGILLIVREY, John 71
MCGREGORY, Dan 123
MCKAY, John 112 125
MCKENZIE, George 68 108 John
   108 140 Wm 139 140
MCKICKAN, Dugald 112
MCNABNEY, James 8 Mrs 9
MCNUT, Rob 112
MCNUTT, John 78 Robt 125
MCTEAR, Mr 17
MELLICHAMP, Mr 62 Thomas

MELLICHAMP (continued)
118
MEPHERSON, Wm 123
MERCHANT, Samuel 122
MEREDITH, Ed 112 Edw 125 Edward 95
MERICK, William 43
MICHAEL, John Car 104
MICHIE, James 25 90 101 139 Joseph 66
MICHO, Abr 125
MIDDLETON, Arthur 8 32 72 Sol 123 William 73
MIKEY, Alexander 134
MILES, Jeremiah 68 71 Thomas 71 William 71 Wm 112
MILLER, Jeremiah 118 Joseph 14 35 38 53 Judith 59 Robert 67 Steven 69
MILLICHAMP, Mr 1 Thomas 126 132 134
MILNER, Jeremiah 56
MISHY, James 71
MITCHEL, Geo 125
MITTCHEL, John 122
MONCE, Thomas 66
MONCK, Tho 2 Thomas 68
MONCKS, Thomas 66
MONGER, Jane 123 Mr 82 Mrs 15
MONGIN, David 125 Priscilla 117
MONIGNAULT, Gabriel 115
MONK, Thomas 74
MONTEITH, John 21
MONTJOY, Mrs 18
MONY, Roger O 104
MOODY, Dr 41 Joseph 29 44 87 99 115
MOON, Jacob 93 118
MOORE, Capt 53 James 73 John 9 17 20 45 72 Justina 71 N 55 Nathaniel 55 Roger 63 128 William 53
MORGAN, 126 Anne 7 Capt 99 Eliz 47 Elizabeth 49 Joseph 15 Joshua 40 47 49 126 134 136 Mr 80 Richard 115 Will 60 William 75 Wm 47
MORLEY, 36
MORPBEW, Mr 63
MORRIS, Anna 113 Edw 113 Samuel 125
MORRISON, Mr 78 Thomas 19

MORRITT, Rich Tho 125
MORTIMER, John 3
MOTT, Mr 86
MOTTE, Jacob 18 22 37 39 Mr 101
MOULTRIE, Dr 99
MOURGUE, Peter 60
MOVERLY, William 89
MUFFINS, Abraham 6
MUIRAIN, Mr 105
MULATTO, Franke 70 James 31 Jamey 117 Mulatto Jemmy 66
MULLINS, Mr 84
MULLRYNE, John 74
MULRAIN, Mr 116
MURPHY, James 107
MURRAY, Mrs 55 Peter 55
MURRELL, Fra 125
MUSGRAVE, John 40
MUSGROVE, J 123 Mr 65
MUSTEE, Diana 11 Phillis 10 Virtue 117
NAPIER, William 19
NASH, Wm 126
NATHAN, John 34
NEAL, Mr 14 24
NEALE, James 31 83
NEGRO, Aaron 19 Abraham 124 Amoretta 10 Amy 138 Anselm 40 Beavour 40 Bella 84 Ben 110 Berwick 128 Besam 99 Bess 92 Betsy 7 92 Betty 4 Boston 92 Brilla 77 Bristol 59 69 92 114 Caesar 92 132 Cafar 130 Caffe 16 Casar 142 Cato 83 95 101 Charles 116 Clarinda 12 Coffee 124 Cojo 89 Cupid 86 Cussie 40 Cussy 92 Cyrus 89 142 Daphne 96 Delia 12 Derry 104 Diana 52 113 Dinah 92 Dirk 118 Dorothy 92 Dublin 60 80 Esham 99 Exeter 99 Filledy 108 110 Flanders 108 Flora 88 Frank 92 George 104 110 Grittah 92 Guam 142 Hagar 92 Hampshire 46 Hanna 74 102 Hannah 102 Harry 26 90 113 Hector 60 Hercules 22 89 Incky 24 Issac 117 Jack 85 92 135 Jackson Hercules 10 Jacob 75 Jeffery 92 Jeney 119 Jenny 92 Joe 12 John 34 Juba 45 Juno

NEGRO (continued)
52 Justice 99 Kate 41 119
Landon 98 Lilly 92 London 4
128 Lubb 110 Lucy 92 Mingo
26 35 89 Moll 101 Nanny 92
Norwich 35 Obbah 99 Ocipio
124 Orinda 48 Owen 6 Paris 92
Parris 61 66 Pendar 113 Peter
38 60 Peter River 110 Phillip
113 Pompey 50 Primus 33 44
84 92 117 130 Prince 86 92
Quash 63 66 Quaw 132 Ryan 2
Sam 92 132 Sambo 18 132
Sampson 82 Sarah 10 Satyra
130 Shadwell 113 Smyrna 83
Solo 125 Sophy 92 Steven 142
Susannah 92 Syphax 44
Taruzen 92 Titus 100 Tom 92
129 Tommy 132 Tony 12 88 92
110 117 Tower-Hill 23
Trampoes 125 Venture 44 Will
133
NERI, Mr 132
NESBETT, Alex 97
NEWBLE, Benjamin 80
NEWTON, John 72
NICHOLAS, George 41 120 131
143
NICHOLLS, Issac 42
NICHOLS, George 73 Issac 72
Nathanial 59
NICHOLSON, Capt 109
NISBETT, Alex 130 Alexander 52
128 Mr 18
NORTH, Edward 69
NORWOOD, James 96
ODINFELLS, Charles 39
OGLETHORP, 48 James 34 54 Mr
40
OGLETHORPE, James 65 Mr 51
63
OLDFIELD, John 17
OLIVER, Geo 125 George 37 Mrs
11 37 Peter 79 98 Wilheim 89
William 89
OLLIER, Mrs James 27
ORDE, Edward 47
OSBORN, William 130 134 Wm
96
OSBORNE, Helena 8 William 8
OSGOOD, Tho Sr 121
OSMOND, 113 134 James 50 Mary

OSMOND (continued)
8 Mr 8
OUIDFIELD, John 73
OULCOTT, Joseph 71
OULDFIELD, J 112 John 8 John
Sr 73
OUODEINTELIS, Capt 71
OWEN, Mrs 132
PADGETT, Peter 73
PAGE, John 42 William 32
PAGETT, Peter 124
PAINE, James 42 60 65 Mr 60
PAINTER, Naomi 41
PALMER, Col 79 123 Francis 121
John 32 51
PAMOR, Eliz 113 123
PANTON, Mr 102 104
PARIS, Alexander 73 Col 71
PARISTON, John 73
PARKER, Cha 123 Ja 123 Mr 38
77
PARRIS, Alex 100 123 Alexander
8 21 106 113 Col 37 130 John
131
PARROCK, Elizabeth 98
PARSONS, Samuel 83
PARTRIDGE, Mrs 47 Wm 130
PATTISON, Joseph 91
PAUL, Capt 52 70 William 70 77
PAULEY, Anthony 71
PAWLEY, Geo 113 Percival 115
125
PAWSY, George 71
PAYNE, Capt 70 Ephm 123
James 71 John 7 140 Peter 95
134
PEACH, Mr 13 Mrs 17
PEARCE, Jeremiah 44
PEIRAY, Hugh 122
PEMBLE, John 27
PENROSE, Bar 110 Bartholomew
79
PEPPER, Daniel 81 143 Mary 100
PERCUNEAU, Alexander 37
Henry 37
PERCY, Hugh 89 121
PERONNEAU, Henry Jr 39
PEROREAU, A B 71
PERRONEAU, Charlest 140 Hen
Jr 50 Henry 125 Sam 125
PERRY, Ben 113 Fr 113 Francis
72 John 119 Mary 119 Rich 122

PERRYMAN, Eliz 113
PETERS, J 123 Wm 112
PETRY, John 76
PETTY, John 87
PHAREUR, John 97
PHILIPS, Eleazer 13 Tho 2
PHILLIPS, Ebenezer 59 Eleazer
   78 104 111 Eleazor Jr 104
   Elezar 34
PHIPP, John 125
PHYPS, John 121
PICK, Capt 15 19 93 95
PICKERING, Mr 18 Mrs 23
PIERCE, Brabazon 51 John 72
PIFBREANE, Mr 128
PIKE, Mary 11 52
PILSON, Thomas 2
PINCKNEY, Charles 3 5 14 16 19
   33 34 36 47 48 54 68 73 82 95
   98 111 115 122 126 127 130
   134 139 Cl 102 Mr 49 89 William 14 18 23 96 111 120 138
   141 Wm 35 47 91
PINDERGRAS, Edward 117
PINDLOCK, James 125
PITTEY, John 82
PLOCK, James 32
POINSET, Mr 114
POINSETTE, Mr 74
POINTSETT, Trooper 8
POLLIXFEN, Robert 120
POLLIXSEN, Capt 122
POOL, Wm 32
POPSON, Joseph 61
PORCHER, Issac 71 73 Peter 71
POREY, Peter 75
PORTAIL, Mr 131
POSTELL, James 41
POWELL, Tho 125 William 80
PREALOW, Joseph 124
PRECOUR, Peter 41
PRIBER, Mr 142
PRINGELL, Jane 77 Robert 77
PRINGLE, Andrew 98 Robert 60
   66 70 98 141
PRIOLEAU, Col 5 12 Samuel 31
   73 126
PROCTOR, Capt 19 Stephen 1 3
   52
PURKIS, John 26 70
PURRY, Col 125 J 112 John Peter
   28 Peter 28

PURRYS, Col 87
QUELCH, Mr 8
QUIXOT, Capt 129
RAGG, John 68
RAMSEY, Col 56 John 78 85 Mr
   85 Mrs 38 60
RANCE, Wedington R 2
RANDAL, Mr 20 William 47
RAVEN, Eliz 123 John 50
RAVENAL, Rene 137
RAVENEL, Rene 31
RAVENELL, Don 105 Renee 71
RAWLINGS, James 46
RAWLINS, Ja 125
RAYPOR, Mr 68
REED, Daniel 129 John 118
REID, James 91 138
REILY, Bryan 104
REMMBERT, Andrew 72
REYNOLDS, John 127
RHODES, Robert 83
RICH, Silvanos 72
RICHARDS, James 23 John 22 45
RICKS, Richard 61
RIDLEY, John 132
RIGG, Alex 97 Alexander 18 38 87
   137 John 18 38 87 97 137 Mr
   37 Samuel 17
RIVERS, George 125 John 87
   Thomas 87 William 82
ROBERT, Peter 23 72
ROBERTS, B 112 John 95 Peter
   117
ROBERTSON, Peter 31 86 Robert
   86
ROBINSON, Robert 89 121
ROCHE, Jordan 33 82 Jourdan 64
ROE, Richard 45
ROGER, Mr 91
ROGERS, Bert 142 James 88 William 93
ROICKLES, Richard 74
ROLFE, George 16
ROLLINS, Mr 76
ROMSEY, John 129 Martha 15
   Mrs 125 Widow 25 Wm 21
ROPER, Jeremiah 21 Mr 95
   Robert 38 45 William 69 77
   131
ROSE, Thomas 91 99
ROUFLARN, James 13
ROUSE, Mr 68

ROUSHAM, James 11
ROWE, Richard 9
ROWLAND, Philip 32
ROWLINGS, James 74
RUSS, John 122 125 Mr 61
RUSSEL, Stephen 34 Wm 38
RUSSELL, Charles 73 85 James
  98 Stephen 82
RUSSIAT, Thomas 15
RUTLEDGE, Andrew 4 73
RYAN, Thomas 80 97
SACHEVEREI, Thomas 115
SAINT JOHN, Ja 125 James 12 23
  47 108 130 Mr 66 70
SAINT JULIEN, Paul de 121
  Peter Day 73
SALTER, Mr 21 Mrs 48
SALTOR, Mr 20
SALTUS, Henry 41 101
SANDERS, Barry 115 John 89
  Laurence 59 Lawrence 38
  Samuel 121 William 52 53 72
  Wm 112 123
SARRAZIN, Moreau 53 93 Mr 118
SATLER, Mr 95
SATUR, Abraham 121 Jacob 9 23
  25 27 63
SAUNDERS, Lambert 32 R 103
  129 Roger 55 73 75 William 73
  Wm 125
SAUREAN, Mary 44
SAUREAU, Mrs 18 20
SAURREAU, Mrs 36
SAVAGE, Benj 114 119 120 125
  Benjamin 34 72 74 89 95 100
  140 Mr 111 113
SAVINEAU, James 49
SAVY, John 28
SAXBY, Mr 11 W 1 William 73
  Wm 25 Wm Sr 125
SAXON, John 18
SCALE, John 71
SCALY, Joseph 71
SCHENCKINGH, Benjamin 39 41
SCONELL, Dennis 127 128
SCOT, Capt 38
SCOTT, Jonathan 140 Mr 139
  Robert 83 William 14 78 129
SCREVEN, Elisha 91 Eliz 125
  Sarah 29 William 72 Wm 123
SCRIVEN, Sarah 37 Widow 42
SCRULL, Edw 8

SCULL, Mr 64
SEABORN, Capt 11
SEABROOK, John 32 Jos 123
  Joseph 50
SEALE, J 113
SEAMAN, 140 Capt 85 George 85
SEARLES, James 12
SECARE, Peter 104
SERJANT, Rowland 135
SERJEAN, Rowland 142
SERRE, Noah 72
SERVANT, Eowen 68
SESION, Thomas 55
SHACKLEFORD, William 72
SHADDOCK, Samuel 17
SHARMOND, George 79
SHAW, Isabelle 61 Peter 15 18
  Robert 79 83
SHEPARD, Mr 95 97 100 104 110
SHEPHEARD, Ch 108 Charles 64
  139 Mr 62
SHEPHERD, John 31 53
SHEPPARD, Charle 68 John 81
  116 120 135
SHREWSBURY, Edward 65 91 Mr
  96 113
SHUBRICK, Capt 86 Rick 56
SHUSTE, 133
SHUTE, Joseph 50 108
SILVER, Jeremiah 13
SIMMONS, Ebenezer 114 John 38
SIMPSON, Edw 48 49 Edward 23
  25 52 86
SINCKLER, John 77 Robert 77
SINCLAIR, Robert 13
SINCLEAR, Ja 125
SINGLETARY, Jos 125
SINGLETAY, Johnathan 71
SINGLETON, Ebenezer 17 Wil-
  liam 72
SINKLER, Alexander 104
SIRRET, William 74
SKEENE, Alexander 72 John 73
SKENE, A 6 Alex 25 Alex Jr 23
  Alexander 16 25 45
SKUTE, Joseph 26 75
SLEIGH, Joseph 50
SLUTE, Jos 114 Joseph 70
SMALL, Edward 10 Sam 115
SMALLWOOD, James 44 68 103
  105 111 138 Mathew 100 Mr 68
SMITH, Alex 38 122 Alexander 19

SMITH (continued)
35 53 Benj 117 Charles 114
Christopher 59 84 106 Col 80
Emanuel 71 Emmanuel 136
Geo 69 George 73 100 Gunpow-
der 56 James 14 John 31 56
Josiah 97 Lamedan 6
Lamgrave Thomas 73
Landgrave 33 66 71 117
Landgrave Thomas 65 Mary 14
Mikell 28 Mr 76 Nich 83 Peter
101 Rich 107 Richard 72 109
130 Rob 25 Samuel 10 119
Sarah 28 Thomas 9 12 19 73
SMYTH, James 56
SMYTHIES, Sergeant 88
SNOW, John 125 Nath 125
Thomas 21 Wm 125
SOMERS, Joseph 5
SOMERVILLE, Mrs 111 Sarah 62
67 Tweedie 5 25 Twiedie 62
SOMMERS, George 110
SPENCER, Alex 82 Anthony 88
William 72 98
SPLATT, Jack 125 John 71
SPOKE, Jonas 31
SPRING, John 104
SPRY, Ryal 110
SQUIRE, Tho 9
STANYARN, Jos 122 Joseph 5
STEED, Edward 19
STEPHENS, Eliz 35 John 67
STERLAND, William 94
STEVEN, John 121 Samuel 50
STEVENS, John 99 Richard 72
STEVENSON, John 101 111 115
133 Mary 106 111 133
STEWART, Alexander 6 J 112 Ja
125 James 55 92 John 112 125
Matthew 68 Robert 137
STILES, Benj 125
STIRLING, William 75
STITSMITH, Anne 69 Mr 32
Thomas 26 69 Ths 32
STOBE, James 64
STOBO, Arch 123 Rob Archb 25
Wm 25 67
STOCKDELL, Perregrine 38
STOCKS, Samuel 113
STOLL, Justinus 28
STONE, Mr 13 Wm 140
STORY, Eliz 139 John 101

STOURSBOROUGH, Luke 65
STOW, Mrs 112 Widow 4
STRAHAN, John 41
STREET, Wm 112
STROBY, William 74
STUART, Adam 115 John 138
STUBBS, Thomas 46
SUMMERS, Ja 112 John 71
Joseph 5
SUMMERVILLE, Sarah 74
SUMNER, Nathaniel 66 Roger 66
SUNDERS, Joshua 108
SUREAU, Fra 125 Mr 82
SURROW, Mrs 2 23
SUTAR, Abraham 16 Jacob 16
SUTHERLAND, Ja 125 John 112
SUTTON, James 62
SWAN, Samuel 77
SWANN, Mr 62
SWEENEY, Miles 71
SWEETMAN, Mr 85
SWETMAN, Mr 124
SWINTON, Hugh 4 115 125 Wil-
liam 6 54 71 Wm 25 122 125
SYMONDS, Capt 75
TALLY, Alexander 97
TANNER, John 23
TAYLOR, Capt 78 James 4 Peter
73 115 Robert 71 105 Sabina
135 Thomas 135
THOMAS, Edw 125 Edward 73 110
113 Wm 125
THOMPSON, Capt 51 105 Ja 123
James 71 John 87 John Jr 31
32 Thomas 49 141 Will 27
THOMSON, James 98
THORNTON, Mr 60
TIDMARSH, Mr 40 110 Richard
115
TIMOTHEE, L 60
TIMOTHY, L 142 Lewis 67 98
107
TIPWORTH, Wm 133
TITTSMITH, Ann 113 Tho 122
TODD, Samuel 96
TOOD, James 85
TOOMER, Hen 112 Henry 135
Henry Jr 134 John 83
TOPHAM, Christopher 135
TOTNEL, Thomas 31
TOWNSEN, Daniel 62
TOWNSEND, J 3 64 Joseph 65 66

TOWNSEND (continued)
91 Mary 64 Mr 99
TOWNSENDS, Daniel 24
TOY, Capt 140
TOZER, Solomon 81 115
TRADD, Mr 18 Robert 41
TRENCH, Alexander 18 27 33
TREWIN, William 82
TRIP, S E 42
TROTT, Mad 102 Madam 12 Mr
17 Nicholas 40 111 Sarah 40
111
TROWELL, Thomas 31 35
TUCKER, J 125
TURNBULL, James 75
TURNER, Joshua 118
TURPIN, Mathew 129
UNDERHILL, Samuel 90
UNDERWOOD, Sam 126 Samuel
134
VALENTINE, George 2
VALETTE, Mrs 7
VANDERDUSIN, Alexander 73
VANDERDUSSEN, Al 142 Alex 48
116 Alexander 12 34 76 105 Mr
7 125 142
VANDERHOEFT, J 123
VANDERHORST, J 112
VANDROLARST, John 36
VANVELSEN, Gerret 137 Mr 1
VANVELSON, Edward 83
VARAMBAUT, Dr 22
VARNER, Elizabeth 125
VARNOD, Widow 70
VAUGHAN, John 102 Mr 45 88
Rowland 24 45 47 60 65 83 87
114 116 119 121 125
VAUGHANS, Rowland 136
VAUGHN, John 74 Rowland 9
VAUGHNS, Rowland 27 28 42
VERGES, Peter 7
VERPLANCK, William 119
VIART, Lydia 62 140
VICARAGE, John 71
VICARIDGE, J 67 141 John 108
VIDEAU, 33
VILLEPONTOUX, Peter 53 82
VINCENT, George 125 Samuel 25
VISSER, Thomas 136
VITTREY, Capt 99
VONRECK, Mr 63 65
WAINWRIGHT, John 55

WAISTLER, Richard 61
WAITES, Wm 115
WALKER, Christopher 32 George
41 James 26 72 Rich 10
Thomas 49 133 138
WALLACE, 109 112 113 140
Walter 106 William 130
WALLIS, John 53
WALPOLE, Horatio 56
WALTER, J 75 John Jr 73 John
Sr 73 William 73
WALTERS, John 118 Joseph 53
WARD, Eliz 125 Samuel 59 Sarah
33
WARHAM, Mr 141
WARING, Mr 118 Thomas 45
WARINGSAN, Benj 117
WARKEM, Charles 87
WARNOCK, Abr 125 Mr 122
WARREN, Peter 7
WARRING, Benjamin 73 Richard
73 Thomas 72
WATERLAND, Wm 87
WATIES, Col 70 Wm 112
WATKINS, William 63
WATKINSON, Capt 12 William
36 41
WATSON, Isabella 96 John 64 91
99 132 137 Joseph 96 Mr 95
William 75 Wm 66
WATSONE, John 107 113
WATTER, John 23
WAY, Jos 112 Joseph 111 Moses
121 Thomas 66 88 101
WEATHERICK, Elizabeth 29
WEAVER, Lucy 132 Sarah 132
Tho 131 Thomas 82 87
WEBB, Sarah 42 43 Will 10 Wil-
liam 4
WEBBER, Sam 113
WEEKLEY, Edward Sr 116 Tho
116
WEEKLY, Wm 137
WELL, Allen 132
WELLS, Edgar 17 John 88 Silas
72
WELSBUYSEN, Daniel 44
WELSH, James 28 Mungo 17 43
William 11
WELSHD, Mrs 61
WELSHUISEN, Daniel 73
WELSHUYEN, Daniel 99

WELSHUYSEN, Dan 123 125
　　Daniel 66 77
WELSHUYSSIN, Daniel 22
WELSHYUSON, Dan 25
WELTHD, Mrs 61
WESKOT, John 122
WEST, Sarah 115 125
WESTBERRY, William 71
WESTBURY, Mr 135 Tho 125
WESTLEAD, Mr 14
WESTON, Edward 64
WETERBURN, James 73
WETHERSPOON, John 25
WHATNELL, John 82
WHIPPY, John 108
WHITAKER, Benj 69 105 116 130
　　132 Benjamin 2-4 14 16 21 27
　　33 35 103 109 Mr 70 141
WHITE, Amth 123 Anthony 79 86
　　John 19
WHITEMARSH, Thomas 1
WHITFIELD, John 101 108 119
　　Rob 112
WHITMARSH, Thomas 66
WICKHAM, Benjamin 89 Maj 40
　　41 Nath 132
WICKHAN, Nathanial 62
WICKING, Elizabeth 108
WICKOM, Nathaniel 73
WIGFALL, Samuel 73
WIGG, Edw 67 Edward 7 Richard
　　33 133 Thomas 6
WIGGFALL, Mr 81
WILKINS, Jonathan 74 William
　　82 William Jr 5
WILKINSON, Joseph 51
WILKS, James 18 23 Joe 110
　　Joshua 123
WILLIAM, Susannah 125
WILLIAMS, John 5 73 Joseph 134
　　Mr 12 Sam 123 Susanna 112
　　Thomas 32
WILLIAMSON, Manley 141 Wil-
　　liam 71 Wm 39
WILLKUYSEN, Daniel 121
WILSON, Elizabeth 79 Hugh 61
　　John 81 Joseph 93 William
　　135
WILTON, William 135
WINDRASS, W 10
WINFIELD, John 133
WIRE, Hugh 98

WITHERS, James 116 John 93
　　Laurence 97 Lawrence 121
WITHERSPOON, John 79 Ruth 90
WITTEN, Tho 123
WITTER, J 113
WITTERBURN, J 74
WOLFORD, Jacob 70
WOOD, Alex 15 28 Hen 113 Henry
　　138 John 3 Mary 3
WOODROP, Wm 133
WOODWARD, John 116 Mary 138
　　Mrs 10 Richard 4 18 86 116
WOOLFORD, Jacob 10 12 96 Mr
　　60 103
WORREL, Mary 23
WORSTED, Christopher 140
WRAGG, Joseph 47 52 53 61 63
　　72 86 108 117 126 130 Mr 32
　　83 99 Sam 67
WRIGHT, Charles 48 James 139
　　Jermyn 48 John 4 56 67 110
　　Richard 56 57 66 67 73 87 110
　　122 125 132 133 Robert 5 25 45
　　47 72 132 Robert Jr 73 Tho 132
　　Thomas 125
WYSS, George 63
YANAM, Fr 98
YEER, Mrs 86
YEOMAN, 10 William 142 Wm
　　115
YEOMANS, 86 89 Mr 106 120
　　William 16 36 133 Wm 81 83
　　123
YOAKLEY, 88
YOMANS, Mr 78 William 79
YONGE, Francis 45 72 82 83
　　Henry 67 71 Lydia 83 Pr 98
　　Robert 83
YOUNG, Archibald 65 John 132
　　Mr 39 Robert 73
ZWILFIER, Dr 65
_____, Frank 118

www.ingramcontent.com/pod-product-compliance
Lightning Source LLC
Chambersburg PA
CBHW071130280326
41935CB00010B/1166